# CHICAGO
# POLICE AND FIRE RETIREMENT GUIDE

★★★★

*UPDATED FOR 2025*

# CHICAGO

## POLICE AND FIRE RETIREMENT GUIDE

## (2ND EDITION)

★ ★ ★ ★

ILLINOIS PUBLIC PENSION FUND ASSOCIATION

FOREWORD BY
JAMES MCNAMEE
PRESIDENT

WINDY CITY
PUBLISHERS

# Chicago Police and Fire Retirement Guide
2nd Edition



Windy City Publishers
www.windycitypublishers.com

Printed in the United States of America

ISBN (2nd Edition):
978-1-953294-63-0

Library of Congress Control Number:
2023922631

Cover Image:
Photo courtesy of Officer Frank Alatorre, Chicago Police Department

Windy City Publishers
Chicago

To all CPD and CFD,
active, retired, and departed
who have taken and kept
a solemn oath to protect others.

**Illinois Public Pension Fund Association**

*An Association of Public Pension Funds*

2587 Millennium Drive, Unit C

Elgin IL 60124, 630-784-0406

www.ippfa.org

# CONTENTS

## DISCLAIMER

Public pensions, Social Security benefits, and deferred compensation arrangements are created and governed by laws. Such laws are subject to change and interpretation. The material in this book is presented solely for educational purposes to supplement and illuminate the information available to you from the only definitive sources: state and federal law. IPPFA, the contributors and the publisher are not offering legal or tax advice, or any other professional service. The reader should not make any decision that effects his or her retirement benefits without consultation with the retirement board, the Social Security Administration, a deferred compensation company's credentialed agent, an attorney, a certified public accountant, or similarly qualified professional.

## INFORMATION APPEARING ELSEWHERE

Some of the information presented appeared earlier in books by IPPFA project coordinator and author Dan Ryan. Permission has been given to use this information in this retirement guide for Chicago fire and police, but the writings were solely created by the authors and are the property of the authors.

## GENDER REFERENCES

Public safety careers are no longer only filled by men. Efforts have been made to make the content of this book gender neutral. When the phrase "he" is used, it is done sparingly and only for the purpose of conversational flow of the text.

## BULK PURCHASES

This book is available on Amazon.com and by bulk purchase (minimum 10 copies) from the IPPFA Office. Contact us at (630) 784-0406 to inquire about bulk purchases or visit our website at IPPFA.org under "Quick Links" at the bottom right corner of the home page.

# FOREWORD

SINCE 1985, THE ILLINOIS PUBLIC Pension Fund Association (IPPFA) has committed time and resources to assist local fire and police pension boards in administering benefits and investing funds to help public safety professionals achieve a secure retirement.

Along the way, we expanded our efforts to ensure that individual members had the ability to maximize their own retirement security and success. As part of that effort, in 2021 we published a retirement income guide for suburban and downstate Illinois police and firefighters.

This book is another tool in that ongoing effort. It brings together much of the information needed to understand and fully utilize benefits available to Chicago police officers and firefighters. We trust that it will fulfill every reader's needs.

Importantly, this 2025 version includes a revised chapter on Social Security, incorporating the changes in the Social Security Fairness Act. This law greatly impacts the Social Security benefits that most Illinois fire and police personnel will receive, including CPD and CFD retirees.

Please remember that beyond this information, there is no limit to the opportunity to expand your personal knowledge of both the financial aspects of life after you stop working as well as the non-financial issues that you may face in retirement. Public sources (books, articles, websites, *etc.*) on these matters are virtually unlimited. Don't let your pre-retirement and post-retirement education end with this book.

And a great source is your pension fund offices, the Chicago Police Annuity and Benefit Fund (Chipabf.org) and the Chicago Fire Annuity and Benefit Fund (Fabf.org). Your retirement funds have full-time professional staff, excellent websites and trustees who are recognized throughout the state and the country as leaders in public safety retirement.

Note that at the time of publication, there is discussion about necessary changes in the benefit levels for Tier 2 retirees—those workers who first became CFD or CPD sworn personnel after January 1, 2011. When you begin to seriously consider your retirement income, please check with the Chicago FABF or PABF pension funds to verify your Tier 2 benefit levels.

Finally, and most importantly, thank you for your commitment to the safety of the City of Chicago.

~James McNamee
President
Illinois Public Pension Fund Association
February 2025

# INTRODUCTION

## YOUR RETIREMENT INCOME IS DIFFERENT

Retirement income is often said to resemble a three-legged stool. It may consist of a pension, Social Security, and your personal savings. Each of the three legs, in your case, is different than the retirement structure of a private-sector worker.

Like you, a neighbor who works at Motorola® or a brother who is a union plumber have pension plans that contribute to retirement security. But their pension plans are formed and governed under the federal Employee Retirement Income Security Act (ERISA). The Pension Benefit Guarantee Corporation (PBGC) provides a base level of insurance should their private sector plans become insolvent. The Board of Trustees has broad latitude to set benefits. It is unlikely that there is any payroll deduction to fund a portion of the benefit—the plan is fully paid for by the employer. There are strict rules protecting the pension rights of spouses, both those married to the pensioner and those who are divorced.

As for *your* pension, the environment and structure are very different. Chicago police and fire pensions are *not* governed by ERISA or insured by any federal agency. Your pension trustees do not set benefits; the State of Illinois does. There is no pension "plan"—there is a pension law adopted by the legislature and signed by the governor. *And you, the employee, pay a substantial portion of your own pension via payroll deduction*—a fact sometimes missed or understated by politicians, citizens, and the media.

As to other aspects of retirement income, your friends and relatives most likely participate in the Social Security system at work. *You do not.* When you spend thirty years outside of Social Security, your federal benefits are greatly impacted.

Your personal savings rules are also different, at least those that govern tax-advantaged savings at work. Private corporate workers save through a 401(k) plan, charitable and educational groups through the 403(b). You save under Section 457 of the Internal Revenue Code. Over the past decade, Section 457 rules have come very close to the 401(k) structure, but there are still differences. A news story or a public television show on workplace savings may not be fully applicable to you.

The purpose of this book is to explain your retirement benefits as they apply to *you*, Chicago municipal fire and police. We'll look at each leg with emphasis on your unique situation as a sworn Chicago police officer or firefighter.

The first two chapters of this book discuss the Illinois pension systems that provide police and fire pension benefits under Articles 5 and 6 of the Illinois Pension Code.

A chapter follows on Social Security. The good news is that previously there were some specific provisions of federal law that reduced Social Security benefits for City of Chicago employees. Those were eliminated in 2025 under the *Social Security Fairness Act*. This updated version of your *Chicago Police and Fire Retirement Guide* addresses those changes. This will help you better understand the Social Security benefits you might receive from work before your public safety career, part-time during your career, and for work after you leave the fire or police department.

The next chapter covers the opportunities for the "personal savings" leg of your retirement plan made available through Deferred Compensation under Internal Revenue Code Section 457.

This material is concise but thorough. It doesn't cover every law, rule or other element of retirement income, but it does hit the key areas that affect police and firefighters in Chicago. Any questions remaining? Please contact your very capable police or fire retirement boards, Nationwide Retirement Services, or contact us at IPPFA.

Illinois Public Pension Fund Association<br>Elgin, Illinois<br>February, 2025

1

## ARTICLE 5

# CHICAGO POLICE PENSIONS

## OVERVIEW

Police officers employed by the Chicago Police Department receive retirement and disability benefits from the Policemen's Annuity and Benefit Fund of Chicago (PABF). The benefits, fund structure, and required member contributions are all spelled out in Article 5 of the Illinois Pension Code.

This chapter explains the pension benefits payable to police retirees and survivors covered under the Article 5 Chicago Police system. Thanks to the pension "reform" law that created two tiers of benefits in 2011, there is a different level of benefits for officers who were in Article 5 service prior to January 1, 2011, and those first hired on or after that date. Where there is a difference in benefits, the chapter has separate sections. Where benefits are the same (*e.g.*, disability benefits), no distinction is made.

Note that at the time of publication, there is discussion about necessary changes in the benefit levels for Tier 2 retirees—those workers who first became CPD sworn personnel after January 1, 2011. When you begin to seriously consider your retirement income, please check with the Chicago PABF pension fund to verify your Tier 2 benefit levels.

## SERVICE RETIREMENT BENEFITS—TIER 1
### (IN SERVICE PRIOR TO JANUARY 1, 2011)

A Tier 1 Chicago police officer is eligible for retirement benefits at age 50 if he or she has earned 20 years of creditable service. A retirement pension is also payable to persons with less than 20 years of service under some options discussed below.

### TIER 1—Chicago Officer
### Final Average Salary Definition

The amount of salary used to compute a Tier 1 pension for a Chicago officer is the average salary for the highest 48 consecutive months in the last 10 years of service.

As an example, let's look at Officer Anderson, age 56, who retires on January 1, 2024, after 30 years of service. The earnings record for this CPD officer's last ten years is as follows:

| YEAR | WAGES |
|---|---:|
| 2023 | $115,000 |
| 2022 | $111,650 |
| 2021 | $108,400 |
| 2020 | $105,250 |
| 2019 | $102,180 |
| 2018 | $99,200 |
| 2017 | $96,300 |
| 2016 | $93,500 |
| 2015 | $90,800 |
| 2014 | $88,140 |

As expected (but not always), this officer's highest salary is at the end of his career. He earned $440,300 in the last 48 months of CPD employment, for a final average salary of $9,177 per month. His pension will be calculated based on an average salary of $9,177 per month.

## TIER 1—Chicago Officer

### Pension Formula—Pensions with 20 Years of Service

An officer age 50 or more, with 20 years of creditable service, is entitled to a pension equal to 50% of the final average salary as described above. For years of service, or fraction thereof, over 20 years, the officer will receive an additional 2.5% of average salary for each year over 20 years, to a maximum pension of 75% of salary. Interestingly, working one day past your anniversary date gives you a full year of pension service credit once you have attained 20 years of service. So the maximum pension occurs after 29 years and one day of service, not a full 30 years.

For example, our Officer Anderson with an average salary of $9,177 per month and a career of 30 years would receive a pension at age 50 or older (he is already 56) at the maximum allowable rate of 75%, or $6,882 monthly. Again, the formula rounds up partial years of service so an officer who worked 28-1/2 years would receive a pension of 72.5% of pensionable salary.

## TIER 1—Chicago Officer

### Pension Formula—Pensions with Less than 20 Years of Service

An officer who does not attain 20 years of service may still retire with a pension from the Chicago fund under two alternatives, as here described:

***Officer Compulsorily Retired***

An officer who has less than 20 years but at least 10 years of service, and who is retired because he or she attains the compulsory retirement age of 65, is entitled to a pension. That pension amount is equal to 30% of average salary for the first 10 years of service, plus 2% of average salary for each year of service, or fraction thereof, in excess of 10 years. For example, such an officer who has 18 years and six months of service could receive a pension equal to 48% of his or her final average salary.

***Officer Not Compulsorily Retired***

Any other officer who attains 10 years but not 20 years of service may receive a pension at or after age 50 under a feature known as a *Money*

*Purchase Annuity.* Under this approach, a separate calculation is performed for the retiree taking into account his or her contributions to the police pension fund, credit for partial contributions from the City, years of service, and the interest earned. The computed value of this is then annuitized (turned into a monthly payment for life) based on the age at which payments begin. There are no annual increases for this type of pension.

### TIER 1—Increases in Pensions after Retirement

A retired officer is entitled to an annual increase in his or her pension. Members who retire with a minimum of 20 years of service receive an increase of 3% of their original pension after they have been retired for 13 months or the month after they attained age 55, whichever occurs later. This increase is awarded each January 1st thereafter for life.

## SERVICE RETIREMENT BENEFITS—TIER 2
## (Began Service After January 1, 2011)

A Chicago Tier 2 officer is eligible for unreduced retirement benefits after 10 years of service and attainment of age 55. The pension is equal to 2.5% of his or her "final average salary" for each year of service. The "final average salary" is the average monthly salary during the last four years of service (technically, the highest 48 consecutive months within the last 60 months of service). The highest allowable pension is 75% of final average salary.

For example, if an officer has 30 years of service and an four-year final average salary of $103,900 annually, the monthly pension would be $6,493.

If a Tier 2 officer with sufficient service credit wishes to retire prior to age 55, the pension may be started any time after age 50, but with a resulting decrease in the monthly amount. The decrease is 6% annually for each year that the officer receives pension prior to age 55 (proportioned monthly).

Note that the Tier 2 law set the highest salary that can be used for calculation of the final average salary at $106,800. This amount is partially indexed for inflation in the future. As of 2025, this cap had been indexed up to $141,407.

### TIER 2—Increases in Pensions after Retirement

The Tier 2 retiree receives an increase on the January 1st on or after the date that the retiree turns age 60, or the month after the first anniversary of the retirement annuity starting date, whichever is later. The increase in pension is the lesser of 3% or one-half of the annual increase in the Consumer Price Index (but not less than 0%). Then, on each subsequent January 1, the officer will receive an additional increase calculated in the same manner on the original amount of his or her pension.

## DISABILITY BENEFITS

A benefit may be paid to a Chicago officer, regardless of age, if the officer is disabled and unable to return to service in the police department. Different levels of benefits are paid depending upon the nature of the disability. There is no age requirement for a disability benefit.

### Line-of-Duty Disability

An officer who becomes disabled as a result of a specific sickness, accident, or injury incurred in or resulting from the performance of an act of duty is entitled to a duty disability benefit equal to 75% of the salary earned at the time of the disability. This payment may be reduced to 50% of salary if the disabling condition was pre-existing at the time of a disabling event.

#### NOTE

A heart attack suffered in the line of duty is considered to be a line-of-duty injury.

An additional payment is made in the amount of $100 per month for each child under age 18 or each disabled child, as long as the total payment to the disabled officer does not exceed 100% of salary. Note also that as of 2000, the benefit payment to a person who has been on duty disability for at least seven years must be equal to at least 60% of the current salary attached to the rank that the person held while an active officer.

### Occupational Disease Disability

For Chicago officers who have completed ten years of credited service, Article 5 benefits for occupational disease disability are payable should their disability be the result of heart disease and they are not entitled to duty disability benefits. Occupational disease disability benefits are 65% of the salary earned at the time of disability. An additional payment is made in the amount of $100 per month for each child under age 18 or each disabled child, as long as the total payment to the disabled officer does not exceed 75% of salary. The benefit payment to a person who has been on occupational disease benefits for at least 10 years must be at least 50% of the current salary attached to the rank the person held while an active officer.

### Ordinary Disability

An officer who becomes disabled as a result of any cause other than performance of duty or occupational disease is entitled to an "Ordinary Disability" benefit. This benefit is equal to 50% of salary when disabled. These payments continue for one year for every four years of service as a Chicago police officer, up to a maximum of five years of Ordinary Disability payments. As an example, a person with 16 years of police fund service is entitled to ordinary disability benefits for up to four years. Note that service credit continues to be earned while an officer is receiving Ordinary Disability benefits.

### Qualifying for Disability

An officer must be found to be disabled by the Board of Trustees upon review of the medical evidence and an examination by a physician appointed by the Board. Once placed on disability, he or she may be examined annually by a Board appointed physician.

### Disability Conversion at Retirement Age

Upon attaining age 65, any disability benefit being received by a Chicago police officer is converted to a retirement pension based on then current salaries. For the conversion calculation, the time on disability is counted as Creditable Service.

## NOTE

Under certain circumstances, disability benefits may be reduced if the officer receives certain benefits under the worker compensation laws of the State or other types of civil recovery.

## PENSIONS PAID TO CHICAGO POLICE SURVIVORS—TIER 1 (OFFICER IN SERVICE PRIOR TO JANUARY 1, 2011)

Pensions are payable to the surviving spouse of a retiree or active employee. There is no minimum age requirement for a survivor pension. Also, there is no continuing requirement that a surviving spouse remain single in order to receive a pension as long as he or she was married to the participant at the time of his or her death. Alternatively, they must have been married for at least one year if the marriage occurred after retirement or disability.

### TIER 1—Spouse Surviving a Pensioner

When an officer who is receiving a pension dies, the surviving spouse is entitled to receive 50% of the pension the retiree was receiving at the time of death.

### TIER 1—Spouse Surviving an Active Officer/Death Not in the Line-of-Duty

Upon the death of an active or disabled officer who has earned at least 18 months of service credit, the surviving spouse will receive a pension that is the greater of either of the following alternatives. First, the surviving spouse is entitled to 30% of the salary attached to the rank of a first-class patrol officer. Alternatively, if the officer was at least age 50 and had earned 20 or more years of service on the day before his death, the surviving spouse is entitled to 50% of the retirement pension for which the deceased officer would have been eligible *If the decedent had less than 20 years, but at least 10 years of service, the survivor pension is 50% of the pension calculated at 20 years of service.*

### TIER 1—Spouse Surviving an Active Officer/Line-of-Duty Death

Upon the death of an active officer who dies as a result of sickness, accident, or injury incurred and resulting from the performance of an act of duty, the surviving spouse is entitled to a pension equal to 75% of the salary attached to the rank held by the deceased officer on the last date of service. Note that at the time the officer would have turned age 65, the pension amount is based on the increased salary being paid to officers of the same rank as the deceased officer.

### TIER 1—Increases in Survivor Pensions

The law does not provide for an annual increase to the pension received by a survivor of a Tier 1 officer. However, PA 102-844, adopted in 2022, provides that the minimum survivor pension will be 150% of the federal poverty level.

### Survivor Benefits for Children and Dependent Parents

Children and dependent parents of officers who die in active service, on disability, or on pension also may receive benefits. Each minor and handicapped child receives 10% of the salary attached to the first-class officer rank (15% if there is no surviving spouse). Total benefits to all members of the family may not exceed 60% of the first-class officer salary, or 100% of same, if the officer was killed in the line of duty.

If there are no surviving children or spouse, a dependent parent may receive a pension equal to 18% of the salary earned by the officer.

## PENSIONS PAID TO CHICAGO POLICE SURVIVORS—TIER 2 (Began Service After January 1, 2011)

Pensions may be payable to the surviving spouse of a retiree or active employee. Also, although benefits are described below as Surviving Spouse benefits, survivor benefits may be payable to children up to age 18, handicapped children regardless of age, or legally dependent parents when there is no surviving spouse. Note that there is no minimum age requirement for a survivor pension. Also, there is no continuing requirement that a surviving spouse remain single in order to receive a pension.

## TIER 2—Spouse Surviving a Pension Recipient

When an officer who is receiving a pension dies, the surviving spouse is entitled to receive survivor benefits in the amount of 66.67% of the pension the officer was receiving at the time of his or her death.

## TIER 2—Spouse Surviving an Active Officer

Upon the death of an active or disabled officer who has earned at least 10 years of creditable service and was at least age 50, the surviving spouse is entitled to receive survivor benefits in the amount of 66.67% of the pension the officer was entitled to receive at the time of death or 30% of the salary attached to the rank of a first-class patrol officer. For example, the spouse of an officer who died after 22 years of service would receive a pension of 55% of final average salary then reduced to 2/3 of that amount. Continuing the example, if an active officer's pension after 22 years of service would have been $4,500 monthly, the surviving spouse benefit would be $3,000. Upon the death of an officer having less than 10 years of service, no pension is payable. The estate of the officer is entitled to a refund of the officer's pension contributions to the Fund.

Under PA 99-0905 passed in 2016,
line-of-duty death benefits are 75% of final salary.

At the date the deceased member would have turned 65 years old, the survivor pension is converted to the retirement pension that the officer would have received.

## TIER 2—Benefits for Non-Spouses

If there is no surviving spouse, minor children and dependent children may receive the survivor benefit payable.

## TIER 2—Increases in Survivor Pensions

The Tier 2 law provides for an increase in the pensions of survivors in a similar manner to the pensions for retired officers. The first increase occurs on the later of the January after the spouse turns age 60 or the January after the spouse has been collecting benefits for one year.

Under PA 102-844, the minimum survivor benefit
was set at 150% of the federal poverty level.

## ADDITIONAL DEATH BENEFITS—ALL POLICE SURVIVORS

### Reversionary Annuity

Chicago Police PABF allows a retiree to take a reduced pension and then have a portion of his or her pension benefit "revert," or become payable to a surviving spouse or other dependent upon the pensioner's death. This is called a *Reversionary Annuity*. Any payment made to a spouse after the retiree dies is in addition to the surviving spouse benefit that is otherwise payable. If you choose a Reversionary Annuity, the decision cannot be changed.

A retiring officer who chooses a Reversionary Annuity may not reduce his or her own pension by more than $200 per month or elect to provide a Reversionary Annuity of less than $50 per month.

A chart in the pension code (Section 5-132.2), available from the Retirement Fund Office, shows how the annuity works. As an example, if a retiring officer is 56 years old and his wife is 53, his election to reduce his own pension by $200 per month would result in a monthly payment to his wife, upon the death of the retiree, of an additional $770 per month. If she dies before he does, his $200 reduction is cancelled out and his pension goes up $200. However, the retiree does not get back the previously diverted money.

### Death Benefits

In addition to the survivor pensions described above, upon the death of an active, inactive, or retired officer, a death benefit is payable to a designated beneficiary. The amount is $12,000 for active or inactive members who have not yet retired, but that amount is reduced by $400 for every year the member is over age 50. For persons already retired on pension, the death benefit is $6,000.

## EMPLOYEE CONTRIBUTIONS

The pension benefits are partially funded by contributions made by active officers. Public employees, particularly Illinois firefighters and police, pay for a good portion of their own pension.

The Article 5 Chicago Police contribution rate is 9% of pensionable salary (excludes overtime but includes duty availability pay). This amount includes

1.5% for the partial funding of survivor's benefits. If you retire without a qualifying survivor, this survivor portion of your contributions may be repaid to you with interest. Interestingly, this refund may be returned to the Fund plus interest if a retired member wishes to reinstate eligibility for survivor benefits.

Payroll contributions are made "pre-tax" so that the member's paycheck does not go down by the full 9%. When a pension is eventually paid, the pension is taxed and the IRS then gets its money.

An officer who resigns or is discharged and does not have pension rights may receive a refund of contributions. Refunds are eligible for a tax-deferred "rollover" to an Individual Retirement Account or other qualified pension plan that accepts such contributions.

Finally, a $2.50 monthly payroll deduction is made to provide for ordinary (*i.e.* not line-of-duty) death benefits.

## TAXATION OF PENSION BENEFITS

Service and survivor pensions are taxed under the federal tax law. Retirees may elect to have federal tax withheld from their pension checks. Taxation of pensions by state governments is governed by state law and Illinois does not currently tax pension payments. If you retire in another state that does tax pensions, it is probable that your Illinois pension fund will not provide for tax withholding for another state. You will have to make some other arrangements to pay non-Illinois state tax, such as making quarterly payments.

Duty and occupational disease disability benefits are not taxed at the federal level, nor are benefits paid to survivors of line-of-duty deaths.

## CREDITABLE SERVICE

Generally, creditable service is active time served as a police officer in Chicago. Periods that are counted include vacation, leave of absence with pay, military service, and disability for which the police officer receives a disability benefit. Military credit prior to assuming police duties is limited to two years if purchased by the officer.

## RECIPROCITY AND PORTABILITY

Active members who have credit in the Chicago Fire pension system may apply to transfer that credit to the Chicago Police plan. The reverse is also true.

Service earned elsewhere in other Illinois public funds may be transferred to the Chicago Police system under a law known as Senate Bill 2520 (SB 2520). At the time it was adopted in 2009, the law allowed a Chicago police officer to transfer up to 10 years of service credit from the other Illinois pension funds that cover sworn officers: downstate municipal, Illinois Municipal Retirement Fund, the Cook County plan, the Municipal Employee Annuity plan, the Metropolitan Water Reclamation District plan, the State employee plan, and the State University Plan. The application had to be made within one year of the adoption of the law for officers employed by Chicago at that time. For new officers since 2009, application must be made to the Chicago Police fund within two years of the Chicago officer's employment date with the City of Chicago.

The cost of this transfer must be borne by the officer. Credit in the prior fund is terminated if a transfer is made. The Chicago Police fund website has information on this transfer possibility. Be sure to contact the Retirement Fund Office if you have prior service that may transfer to your CPD pension.

A provision of the Illinois Pension Code that expired in 2023 allowed a Chicago police officer to transfer Creditable Service to an Article 3 "Downstate" police pension fund (which included most Chicago suburbs). The cost of this transfer was borne by the officer. That provision is no longer in effect. Another opportunity may be approved by the State Legislature in the future.

## GOVERNANCE

### Legal Creation and Oversight

Illinois law governs your Article 5 pension fund. Federal law plays only a small taxation and disclosure role. The Illinois Pension Code is Chapter 40 of the Illinois Compiled Statutes, 40 ILCS 5, and then the specific pension systems are created and regulated under separate articles. The Policemen's Annuity & Benefit Fund of Chicago is one of those specific pension systems.

## The Board of Trustees and Staff

The Fund is governed by a Board of Trustees ("the Retirement Board") consisting of eight members: three elected active members (one each at the lieutenant, sergeant, and patrol officer ranks), one elected retiree and four trustees appointed by the Mayor. The Trustees have a fiduciary responsibility to govern the Fund in a prudent manner within the requirements and limitations of Illinois law. Meetings are held monthly and are open to the public except when personnel matters are discussed, as allowed by Illinois law. Trustees may not be paid for service as Trustees of the Fund. The Retirement Board holds separate meetings when it acts as a whole as the Investment Committee.

The Fund has a professional staff who assist the Trustees in operating the pension plan and gives aid and guidance to Chicago officers. They have established an excellent website, chipabf.org, that provides summary and detailed information on pension benefits. Most notably, the website has:

- **A Retirement Calculator**. This calculator allows you to estimate your earned and future retirement benefits. Be sure to know if you have any unpaid suspensions before you rely completely on the estimates given.
- **A Participant Handbook**. This handbook provides more information on the retirement and disability benefits than could be provided in this book. It is an excellent source.
- **The Planning for Retirement Page**. This page provides information on how to go about the retirement application process. Note that FOP Lodge 7 has advised IPPFA that a key date for retirement is to apply by September 30th of the year before you wish to retire. The Planning for Retirement Page also provides information on your potential eligibility for continued health insurance through the City of Chicago.
- **Divorce / QILDRO Page**. This page provides information and forms for members going through divorce.

Chipabf.org is a great resource—use it!

## Role of Professional Consultants

To assist the Board of Trustees in carrying out their duties, the Fund retains a qualified actuary, certified public accountant, an investment consultant, a consulting physician, investment managers, and independent legal counsel.

## Role of the Illinois Department of Insurance

The Department of Insurance is authorized under the statutes to create rules governing pension administration, to regulate public pension funds, to audit public pension funds, and to report to the Legislature as to the valuation of these funds. The Public Pension Section handles these responsibilities. The entire department and the pension section are active participants in protecting public employee pensions. They may be contacted at the Public Pension Section, Illinois Department of Insurance, 320 W. Washington St., Springfield, IL 62767.

## Member Data for Participation

To ensure coverage and benefits under the Pension Fund, officers should apply for participation and complete the pension plan's necessary forms. Note that the State of Illinois requires that information on marital status, children, and your birth certificate be kept in the pension fund's records. If your information is always up to date, this will help ensure timely processing of your benefits, especially if a catastrophic event occurs. Also, since it is a requirement of the pension fund that this data be maintained, keeping your records current will help your pension fund when they are examined by the State.

## Administrative Review

Final administrative decisions of the Board of Trustees are subject to judicial review under the Illinois Administrative Review Law.

## WHAT NEXT?

Again, the system's website, chipabf.org, has excellent on-line information for active and retired participants. You can also gain access to the plan's financial information. The audit and actuarial reports are a little tough to digest but are worth the effort for you to learn about your pension fund. Also, the actuarial report has an excellent summary of benefits that you can use to supplement your pension knowledge.

Contact the Chicago Police fund's professional staff or the Trustees assigned to the Retirement Board to assist you with any questions.

The website for the Fraternal Order of Police Lodge 7 has an excellent summary of disability benefits. See chicagofop.org/benefits/disability-benefits.

As a Chicago police officer you are not covered under Social Security for your police work. However, you may have earned Social Security benefits from work outside of the police force. Be sure to read the section of this book on Social Security benefits.

Also, you are eligible to voluntarily save and invest a portion of your salary under the City's Section 457 Deferred Compensation Plan. Read the section of this book on deferred compensation and contact your plan at 1-877-677-3678 for specific information.

2

ARTICLE 6

# CHICAGO FIRE PENSIONS

THE FOLLOWING INFORMATION IS CONTAINED in the Chicago Fire Annuity and Benefit Fund "Summary of Benefits" available on their website, fabf.org. Note that at the time of publication, there is discussion about necessary changes in the benefit levels for Tier 2 retirees—those workers who first became CFD or sworn personnel after January 1, 2011. When you begin to seriously consider your retirement income, please check with the Chicago FABF pension funds to verify your Tier 2 benefit levels.

## SUMMARY OF BENEFITS

The following Summary of Benefits is presented for participants of the Firemen's Annuity and Benefit Fund (the "Fund") for general information concerning the provisions and benefits currently available under the Illinois Pension Code (40 ILCS, Act 5, Articles 1,1A and 6). For the avoidance of doubt, the Illinois Pension Code, and any other applicable law, supersedes anything stated or implied herein. Pursuant to their authority, the Illinois General Assembly may modify the Illinois Pension Code at any time and this Summary of Benefits may contain outdated information that should not be relied on by participants. As such, participants should review the Illinois Pension Code for updated information regarding the benefits available to participants. Participants are also encouraged to contact Fund representatives for specific inquiries as to what benefits may be available for participants and their respective beneficiaries.

## FUND ADMINISTRATION

The Fund is administered by a Board of Trustees called the Retirement Board. It is composed of eight members: four *ex-officios*; the City Treasurer, City Clerk, City Comptroller and Deputy Fire Commissioner, and four persons who must be participants of the Fund; three active participants and one retired participant.

The Retirement Board elects one of its own members as President, one as Secretary and one as Vice President. The Retirement Board is required by law to hold regular meetings each month. These meetings are generally held the third Wednesday of each month. The meetings are open to the public consistent with the requirements of the Open Meetings Act (5 ILCS 120/1 *et seq.*).

Among its other duties, the Retirement Board is required to consider and vote on all applications for annuities and benefits; invest the monies of the Fund within certain prescribed parameters; make rules and regulations for the proper conduct of the affairs of the Fund; contract with an independent certified public accounting firm to perform an annual audit and to issue an opinion on the financial statements of the Fund; submit an annual detailed report of the affairs of the Fund to the City Council; adopt an annual budget and obtain any necessary professional assistance by contract or employment.

Questions concerning a member's individual benefit may be directed to the Fund office by e-mail to info@fabf.org; by phone (312) 726-5823; or in writing to 20 S. Clark St. Suite 1400, Chicago, IL 60603.

## MEMBER DOCUMENTATION

Upon becoming employees of the Chicago Fire Department ("CFD"), Fund participants shall submit the following documentation to the Fund:

- A certified or original copy of their birth certificate.
- Name and birth date of spouse or civil union partner, a certified or original copy of the spouse or civil union partner's birth certificate and a certified or original copy of a marriage certificate or certificate representing a valid civil union.

- Names, birth dates, certified or original birth certificates and formal notices of legal adoption (if applicable) of all children.
- Certified or original copies of divorce decrees or death certificates from any previous marriages of the participant and spouse; and
- Documentation attesting to the disability of any permanently disabled child.

## CONTRIBUTIONS

### Salary & Employee Contributions

Salary throughout this document refers to Career Service Salary and Exempt Rank Salary for participants meeting certain criteria. Each participant's total contribution percentage is currently 9⅛% of salary broken down as follows:

- 7⅛% for Firefighter's Annuity
- 1½% for Spouse's Annuity
- ⅜ of 1% for the Increment after Retirement (Annuity Increment)
- ⅛ of 1% for Ordinary Disability Benefits (this is not refundable)

Beginning January 1, 1999, salary includes the additional compensation payable to participants by virtue of being licensed as an Emergency Medical Technician (EMT). Beginning January 16, 2004, and for any prior periods for which applicable contributions have been paid, salary shall include the classified career service rank of Ambulance Commander. Beginning January 16, 2004, and for any prior period for which applicable contributions have been paid, pensionable salary shall include duty availability pay received by the participant.

Beginning January 16, 2004, for the purpose of computing employee and City contributions, salary means the actual salary attached to the exempt rank position held by the participant. For the purpose of computing benefits, salary means the actual salary attached to the exempt rank position held by the participant if (1) the contributions on the exempt rank salary for all exempt periods after January 1, 1994 have been paid, (2) the participant held an exempt position for at least 5 consecutive years, (3) the participant held the rank of battalion chief or field officer for at least 5 years during the exempt period, and (4) the participant was born before 1955; otherwise salary means the salary attached to the career service rank held by the participant.

Beginning January 1, 2011, for members hired on or after January 1, 2011, the annual salary shall not exceed $106,800; however, that amount shall be increased annually by the lesser of (1) 3% including all previous adjustments or (2) ½ of the annual unadjusted percentage increase (but not less than zero) in the consumer price index-u for the 12-month period ending with the September preceding each November 1st including all previous adjustments. The annual salary cap in 2024 is $138,093, future increases will be posted on the website at www.fabf.org.

## REFUNDS

### Employee Refunds

A participant who resigns or is discharged from service shall be entitled to a refund of their contributions for annuity and spouse's annuity plus interest and the increment increase, provided he is under age 50 (with any length of service) or he is less than age 57 if he has under 10 years of service. The 1/8 of 1% contributions for ordinary disability benefits is non-refundable.

Any participant that receives a refund of contributions and subsequently re-enters service, may re-establish that service credit with the Fund by repaying the refund amount plus interest at the actuarially assumed rate compounded annually, from the date of the refund to the date of repayment within two years after the date of re-entry into service. The Fund will utilize the re-entry date for all purposes under the Code for participants that re-enter service and do not repay refunds of contributions and the required interest within the two-year period provided in the Code.

### Refund of Spousal Contributions

A participant who is unmarried at the time of retirement is entitled to a refund of contributions for spouse's annuity purposes.

Beginning January 16, 2004, the widow of a participant who received a refund of contributions for widow's annuity at the time of his retirement is not eligible for widows benefits unless the refund is repaid to the Fund, with interest at a rate of 4% per year compounded annually, from the date of the refund to the date of repayment. The marriage must exist for at least one year prior to the participant's death for a spouse to be eligible for benefits. Benefits commence upon the death of the participant and receipt of repayment.

## SERVICE CREDIT

### Accumulation of Service Credit

Participants earn service credit in the Fund during all periods in which they perform the duties of their position and all periods of vacation, leave of absence with whole or part pay, leave of absence during which the participant was engaged in the military or naval service of the United States of America, and periods of disability for which the participant receives any disability benefit, provided that the participant elects to make the contributions to the Fund according to the provisions of the Statute.

Any Tier 2 participant shall not be given service credit in this Fund for any period of time in which the member is in receipt of retirement benefits from any annuity and benefit fund in operation in the City.

### Purchase of Additional Service Credits

#### *Service Credit for Periods during Employment*

Participants may opt to purchase additional service credits in certain situations including periods of suspension from duty not to exceed a total of one year during the total period of service of the participant and 1980 strike time not to exceed 23 days in accordance with an agreement with the City on a settlement of the strike. Participants must elect to make the required contributions plus interest in accordance with the provisions of the Statute as though they were an active participant, based upon the salary attached to the career service rank and grade held by the participant during such absence from duty.

No payments for overtime or extra service credit shall be included in computing service of a participant and not more than one year or a proper fractional part thereof of service shall be allowed for service rendered during any calendar year.

### *Service Credit for Prior Military Service*

Active participants that served in the Armed Forces of the United States prior to employment with the CFD may purchase up to 24 months of service credits for pension purposes. There is no deadline for active eligible participants to purchase these credits.

### *Service Credit for Employment with the Chicago Police*

Active participants that were formerly members of the Policemen's Annuity and Benefit Fund of Chicago may transfer service credits earned in the Policemen's Fund to the Firemen's Fund upon application to the Policemen's Fund and payment to the Firemen's Fund of all statutorily required contributions.

### *Other Additional Service Credit*

From time to time the Statute has provided that participants may purchase other periods of service. Participants are encouraged to review the Statute and visit the Fund website at www.fabf.org for more information.

## RETIREMENT BENEFITS

### TIER 1—Retirement Benefits

Tier 1 benefits are for participants who first become a fireman or paramedic under this Article before January 1, 2011. The calculation of a retirement annuity may not exceed 75% of the highest salary received by a participant.

### Minimum Formula Annuities (More Than 20 Years of Service)

Minimum Formula Annuities are payable to Tier 1 participants, that have attained age 50 and have at least 20 years of accumulated service credit, or after December 31, 1990, a participant may withdraw with 20 years of service regardless of their age and receive this annuity upon attainment of age 50.

The calculation of a Minimum Formula Annuity is equal to 50% of the average salary, plus an additional 2.5% of average salary for each year of service or fraction thereof beyond 20 years of service based on the entrance date into the Fund. For purposes of this section, average salary is the highest 48 consecutive months of the last 10 years of service. This service is reduced by any lost time at date of withdrawal. Minimum Formula Annuity benefits may not exceed 75% of such final average salary.

Effective 2022, the minimum annuity for those who have retired from service at age 50 or over with 20 or more years of service shall be no less than 150% of the Federal Poverty Level.

### Alternative Minimum Formula Annuities (More Than 23 Years of Service)

Tier 1 participants are eligible to receive Alternative Minimum Formula Annuities for participants that have attained age 53 and have at least 23 years of accumulated service credit.

The calculation of an Alternative Minimum Formula Annuity is equal to 50% of the average salary, plus an additional 2% of average salary for each year of service or fraction thereof after attaining age 53 with 23 years of service. Each participant who has completed 23 years of service before attaining age 53 shall have an additional 1% of average salary added for each year of service or fraction thereof in excess of 23 years up to age 53. For purposes of this section, average salary is the highest 48 consecutive months of the last 10 years of service. This service is reduced by any lost time at date of withdrawal.

Effective 2022, the minimum annuity for those who have retired from service at age 50 or over with 20 or more years of service shall be no less than 150% of the Federal Poverty Level.

### Earned Annuities (10-20 Years of Service)

Basic vesting in the Fund occurs after 10 years of creditable service. Calculations for Earned Annuities are based upon the amount the participant has contributed to the Fund, partial City contributions, interest, age, and years of service.

Earned or Money Purchase Annuities are payable to Tier 1 participants who have attained age 50 with at least 10 years of service. If a participant has 10 years of service and has not yet attained age 50, his Earned Annuity shall be fixed as of and be computed as if he were exactly 50 and the benefit will be payable upon his attainment of age 50 and upon proper application and Board approval.

### Compulsory Retirement Annuities (10-20 Years of Service)

As of December 31, 2000, the CFD's compulsory retirement age is 65 for firefighters. There is no current compulsory retirement age for paramedics.

Effective January 16, 2004, a Tier 1 participant who is required to withdraw from service due to attainment of compulsory retirement age or is not subject to compulsory retirement age but is at least age 65 at the time of withdraw, and has at least 10 but less than 20 years of service credit may elect to receive an annuity equal to 30% of average salary for the first 10 years of service plus 2% of average salary for each completed year of service or fraction thereof in excess of 10 years, but not to exceed a maximum of 50% of average salary. For purposes of this section, average salary is the highest 48 consecutive months of the last 10 years of service. The participant is entitled to statutory post-retirement increases.

### Automatic Annual Increase (For Tier 1 Participants)

Beginning April 5, 2021, Tier 1 participants retiring with at least twenty years of service will receive an annual 3% increase based on their original annuity amount continuing for their lifetime, contingent upon both of the following conditions being met:

- The participant must have attained age 55
- The participant must have been retired at least one year and one month

If a participant is over 54 when they retire the increment begins the first of the month following the first anniversary of his retirement and again each January 1st thereafter for life.

## TIER 2 RETIREMENTBENEFITS

Tier 2 benefits are for participants who first become a fireman or paramedic under this Article on or after January 1, 2011.

### Monthly Retirement Annuities (More than 10 Years of Service)

Monthly Retirement Annuities are payable to Tier 2 participants who have withdrawn from service, attained age 50 or more, have 10 or more years of service, and have completed a proper application and Board approval.

The calculation of a Monthly Retirement Annuity is equal to 2.5% of average salary for each year of service, subject to an annuity reduction factor of one-half of 1% for each month that the participant's age at retirement is under age 55. For purposes of this section, average salary is the highest 48 consecutive months of salary of the last 5 years of service. This service is reduced by any lost time at date of withdrawal. Monthly retirement annuities shall not exceed 75% of average salary.

Beginning January 1, 2011, for members hired on or after January 1, 2011, the annual salary shall not exceed $106,800; however, that amount shall be increased annually by the lesser of (1) 3% including all pervious adjustments or (2) ½ of the annual unadjusted percentage increase (but not less than zero) in the consumer price index-u for the 12 months ending with the September preceding each November 1st including all previous adjustments. The annual salary cap for 2025 is $141,407, future increases will be posted on the Fund website at www.fabf.org.

### Automatic Annual Increase (For Tier 2 Participants)

The monthly annuity of a Tier 2 participant shall be increased on the January 1st occurring on or after the later of:

- the attainment of age 60, or
- the first anniversary of the annuity start date

This annuity shall be increased each January 1st thereafter.

Each annual increase shall be calculated at 3% or one-half of the annual unadjusted percentage increase (but not less than zero) in the consumer price index-u for the 12-month period ending with the September preceding each November 1, whichever is less, of the originally granted retirement annuity. If the annual unadjusted percentage change in the consumer price index-u decreases, then the annuity shall not be increased.

## DEPENDENT BENEFITS

### Widow/Widower Annuities

#### *Eligibility Requirements*

Eligibility for widow and surviving spouse annuities require that the spouse be married to the Active/Retired participant at the date of his death.

In accordance with Illinois law, civil union partners are eligible for the same benefits as widows and spouses of participants.

### *Marriage on Disability or Retirement*

Beginning January 16, 2004, a widow who married a participant while he was in receipt of disability benefits may be eligible for a widow's annuity provided they were married for at least one year prior to the participant's death.

Beginning January 16, 2004, the widow of a participant who received a refund of contributions for widow's annuity at the time of his retirement is not eligible for widows benefits unless the refund is repaid to the Fund, with interest at a rate of 4% per year compounded annually, from the date of the refund to the date of repayment. The marriage must exist for at least one year prior to the participant's death for a spouse to become eligible for benefits. Benefits commence upon death of the participant and receipt of the repayment.

## TIER 1—Widows/Widower Annuities

Tier 1 widow's annuities are for widows of participants who first become a fireman or paramedics under this Article before January 1, 2011. There are no automatic annual increases for the widows of participants that enter service prior to January 1, 2011.

### *Widows of Members That Die After Retirement*

An eligible widow of a Tier 1 participant that dies after retirement is entitled to receive 50% of the participant's annuity at the time of his death or the minimum widow's annuity allowed by the Statute, whichever is greater. These annuities cease upon the widow's death.

### *Duty Death Widows (Compensation Widows)*

Upon Board approval when a Tier 1 participant is killed in the performance of duty or dies while in receipt of Duty Disability benefits that rendered the participant unable to resume service in the fire department, the widow shall receive 75% of the current annual salary attached to his rank and grade. In order to qualify for the annuity benefits provided for duty death widows, the widow must be married to the fireman at the time of the act or acts of duty which resulted in his or her death consistent with the requirements of the Statute. This benefit is increased proportionately with all future department increases to salary consistent with the applicable provisions of the Statute.

### *Widows of Participants That Die While in Service (Non-Duty)*

If the death of a Tier 1 participant occurs after 1 ½ years of service, the widow's annuity shall be the greater of; (1) 30% of the salary attached to the rank of first class firefighter (minimum of step 6), but does not exceed the final step of the first class firefighter pay scale or (2) 50% of the retirement annuity the deceased participant would have been eligible to receive if he had retired from service on the day before his death and qualified for the minimum formula annuity (age 50 with at least 20 years of service) or, (3) the minimum widow's annuity allowed by the Statute for his or her lifetime.

Effective January 16, 2004, the widow's annuity payable to the widow of a participant who dies on or after July 1, 1997 while an active participant with at least 10 years credible service shall be no less than 50% of the retirement annuity that the deceased participant would have been eligible to receive if he had attained age 50 and 20 years of service on the day before his death and retired on that day.

### *Widows of Participants Withdrawn from Service and Death Prior to Age 50*

If a Tier 1 participant who has resigned from service prior to age 50, with at least 10 years of service dies, his widow is entitled to either an earned widow's annuity or the minimum widow's annuity allowed by the Statute.

### *Minimum Widows Annuities*

Beginning January 1, 2023, the minimum widow's annuity payable to any person who is entitled to receive a widow's annuity under this Article is 150% of the Federal Poverty Level.

## TIER 2—Widow/Widower Annuities

Tier 2 widow's annuities are for widows of participants who first become a fireman or paramedic under this Statute on or after January 1, 2011.

### *Widows of Members That Die After Retirement*

A widow of a Tier 2 participant that was receiving an earned pension at the date of his death is entitled to receive 66 2/3% of the participant's annuity at the time of his death or the minimum widow's annuity allowed by the Statute, whichever is greater.

### *Duty Death Widow (Compensation Widow)*

Upon Board approval when a Tier 2 participant is killed in the performance of duty or dies while in receipt of disability benefits and the act or acts of duty resulted in his death, the widow shall receive 75% of the current annual salary attached to his rank and grade; provided, however, that no such benefit shall be paid to the widow spouse of a fireman who dies while in receipt of disability benefits when the fireman's death was caused by an intervening illness or injury unrelated to the illness or injury that had prevented him from subsequently resuming active service. In order to qualify for the annuity benefits provided for duty death widows, the widow must be married to the fireman at the time of the act or acts of duty which resulted in his or her death consistent with the requirements of the Statute. This benefit is increased proportionately with all future department increases to salary.

### *Spouses of Members That Die in Active Service (Non-Duty Less than 10 Years of Service)*

If the death of a Tier 2 participant occurs after 1 ½ years of service but before 10 years of service, the spouse's annuity shall be 30% of the salary attached to the rank of first-class firefighter in the classified career service at the time of the participant's death or the minimum widow's annuity allowed by the Statute, whichever is greater.

### *Spouses of Members that Die After 10 Years of Service but Before they Begin Retirement*

If the Tier 2 deceased participant was not receiving a pension at the time of his death but had at least 10 years of service, the surviving spouse is entitled to the greater of (1) 30% of the salary attached to the rank of first class firefighter in the classified career service at the time of the participant's death, (2) 66 2/3% of the Tier 2 monthly retirement annuity that the participant would have been eligible to receive based on his actual service but determined as though the participant was at least age 55 on the day before his death or, 3) the minimum widow's annuity allowed by the Statute.

### *Minimum Widows Annuities*

Beginning January 1, 2023, the Minimum Widow's Annuity payable to any person who is entitled to receive a spouse's annuity under this Article is 150% of the Federal Poverty Level.

### *Automatic Increase*

The monthly annuity of a surviving spouse of a Tier 2 participant that died after retirement or with 10 or more years of service shall be increased on the January 1st after (1) attainment of age 60 by the widow, or (2) the 1st anniversary of the Tier 2 widow's annuity start date, whichever is later and each January 1st thereafter.

Each annual increase shall be calculated at 3% or ½ of the annual unadjusted percentage increase (but not less than zero) in the consumer price index-u for the 12-month period ending with the September preceding each November 1, whichever is less of the originally granted annuity.

## CHILD'S ANNUITIES

Minor children of participants who die while in service, on disability, or while receiving an annuity are eligible for children's annuity benefits. The amount of this benefit is equal to 10% of the current annual maximum salary attached to the position of first-class firefighter, for each child as set by the Statute. If there is no surviving parent, these benefits amount to 15% of the same.

This benefit terminates upon the attainment of age 18, marriage, or death. Total benefits paid to all members of a family cannot exceed 60% of the current maximum first-class firefighter salary. This maximum benefit is increased to 100% for the family of a participant killed in the line of duty.

If the child is disabled because of a handicap (and the handicap manifests prior to age 18), upon proper application and documentation, benefits may be available in the same manner as child's annuity benefits and are payable to the parent of such child as the natural guardian, a court appointed guardian, or a special needs trust. Benefits terminate at death, if it is determined that the child is no longer disabled because of the handicap, or if the child marries.

## PARENT'S ANNUITIES

Natural parent(s) of a participant who dies while in active service, on disability, while receiving a minimum formula annuity, or while receiving a monthly retirement annuity may be eligible for parent's annuity benefits provided, that at the time of the participant's death; 1) no widow or unmarried child under the age of 18 years of age are entitled to an annuity under other provisions of the Statute; 2) and that satisfactory proof shall be presented to the Board that the participant was contributing to the support of his parent or parents.

The benefit is equal to 18% of the participant's current annual salary at the time of death or his retirement for each surviving parent.

## DISABILITY BENEFITS

Active participants, removed from the Fire Department payroll due to a medical leave of absence are eligible to make application for duty, occupational or ordinary disability benefits. During all periods of disability, participants shall be treated as though they were active members for retirement and dependent annuity purposes under the Statute.

No disability benefits shall be paid for any period of time for which a participant has a right to receive any part of his salary unless the participant is certified to be terminally ill by a Board-appointed physician and the Board makes a determination that the participant is eligible to receive a benefit. However, active participants may not receive such disability benefit payments at the same time the participant is in receipt of salary. Failure to comply with Board approved policies and the Statute regarding the receipt of a disability benefit may result in suspension and/or possible termination of a disability benefit.

## DUTY DISABILITY

Participants who become disabled as the result of a specific injury, or of cumulative injuries, or a specific sickness incurred in or resulting from an act or acts of duty are eligible for duty disability benefits during any period of such disability.

Duty disability benefits are equal to 75% of the participant's salary on the date of removal from the payroll. This benefit is fixed at the time the participant leaves the Fire Department payroll and is payable until the earlier of death, retirement, or until the participant is removed from his disability status. However, beginning January 1, 1994, no duty disability benefit that has been payable for at least 10 years shall be less than 50% of the current salary attached from time to time to the rank and grade held by the participant at the time of his removal from the department payroll, regardless of whether that removal occurred before the effective date.

The participant's children are also entitled to child's disability benefits in the amount of $30.00 per month per child under age 18 or until the participant is removed from his disability status. If the child is handicapped, the $30.00 is payable until the participant is removed from his disability status. The total amount of the child's disability benefit cannot exceed 25% of salary at the time of the grant.

## OCCUPATIONAL DISABILITY

Participants with a minimum of seven years of credible service that become disabled from heart disease, tuberculosis, any disease of the lungs or respiratory tract, AIDS, hepatitis C, stroke, or cancer resulting from his or her service in the department are entitled to occupational disease disability benefits during any period of such disability.

In order to receive this occupational disease disability benefit, the cancer involved must be a type which may be caused by exposure to heat, radiation or a known carcinogen as defined by the Internal Agency for Research on Cancer.

Occupational disease disability benefits are equal to 65% of the participant's salary on the date of removal from payroll. This benefit is fixed at the time the participant leaves the Fire Department payroll and is payable until the earlier of death, retirement, or the participant is removed from his disability status. However, beginning January 1, 1994, no occupational disease disability benefit that has been payable for at least 10 years shall be less than 50% of the current salary attached from time to time to the rank and grade held by the participant at the time of his removal from the department payroll, regardless of whether that removal occurred before the effective date.

The participant's children are also entitled to child's disability benefits in the amount of $30.00 per month per child under age 18 or until the participant is removed from his disability status. If the child is handicapped, the $30.00 is payable until the participant is removed from his disability status. The total amount of these combined benefits is not to exceed 75% of salary at the time of the grant.

## ORDINARY DISABILITY

Ordinary disability benefits are provided for a participant who becomes disabled as the result of any cause other than duty or occupational disease disabilities and is equal to 50% less 9% (for pension deductions) for a total of 41% of salary on the date of removal from the payroll.

Ordinary disability benefits are payable for a period of half the participant's service, limited to a maximum of five years. Ordinary disability benefits terminate when the disability ceases, after the maximum of 5 years set by the Statute, or when the participant becomes eligible for minimum formula annuity. No children's benefits are payable.

## APPLICATION PROCEDURES

The process of making an application, being evaluated by the Fund's physician, and appearing before the Board for a hearing takes approximately 3 months to complete. Generally speaking, the procedures to make application for disability benefits are:

- Exit interview with CFD Human Resources—At approximately 9 months into the allowed 12-month layup period, CFD members should complete an exit interview with CFD Human Resources, a final review visit at CFD medical, and sign an authorization for release of medical information from CFD to the Fund.
- Make an application for disability at least 2½ months prior to your exit date. You must have an end of employment form from CFD at the time you make application for disability.
- Gather your medical records—Your disability application requires a complete review of your medical records. Sign an authorization for release of medical information to the Fund. It is imperative that all medical records are received at least 6 weeks prior to the hearing.
- Contact with the Fund nurse case manager—The Fund will assign a nurse case manager to assist in the review of your disability claim. Your case manager will contact you via telephone and will assist in obtaining any additional medical records needed. She will schedule your appointment will the Fund's physician as well as any other appointments requested by the Board.
- Meet with the Fund physician—Your appointment with one of the Fund's physicians may be scheduled the same month as your CFD payroll removal date, or sometime thereafter.

- Attend your Hearing—A hearing before the Board will be scheduled after your appointment with the physician as long as all medical documentation has been received in an adequate amount of time prior to your hearing. If additional information is required, the hearing may continue in a subsequent month. At the completion of the hearing(s), the Board votes whether or not to grant the disability benefit application.
- File for Administrative Review—If you dispute the decision, under the provisions of 40 ILCS 5/6-222 and 735 ILCS 5/3-103, you must file for an Administrative Review of the Board's decision within 35 days that the letter was sent to you at your last known residence.

## RE-EXAMS

Participants receiving disability benefits shall be examined at least once a year or longer periods as determined by the Board, by a Board appointed physician. However, the Board has the right to request an examination of any disability participant as deemed necessary. As part of the re-examination process all disability participants who are working are required to submit a job description. When a disability ceases, the Board shall discontinue payment of the benefit.

## MISCELLANEOUS

### Death Benefit

The Fund pays an ordinary death benefit to the designated beneficiary or beneficiaries of deceased participants. For active participants in receipt of salary at the time of their death age 49 and under, the death benefit amounts to $12,000 and is reduced by $400 for each year over age 49 to a minimum of $6,000. A participant on disability is treated as though he were in active service in this regard. Eligible beneficiaries for participants retired after January 1, 1962, in receipt of retirement benefits, and whose separation from service (active duty) was effective on or after the participant's attainment of age 50, and application for such annuity was made within 60 days after separation from service (active duty), receive $6,000.

## Health Insurance

The City of Chicago collects 1.45% of annual salary for a participant's coverage in Medicare for all employees hired after April 1, 1986.

The Fund serves only as a conduit to collect and forward payment of premiums authorized by the participant from the participant's benefit check to eligible health care plans. The authorization forms necessary to process such payment of health care premiums are available on the Fund's website at www.fabf.org.

All questions concerning eligibility or plan coverage should be directed to the healthcare plan provider.

## Military Benefits

In compliance with 40 ILCS 5/1-118, the Fund shall comply with the requirements of the federal Uniformed Services Employment and Reemployment Act ("USERRA") the federal Heroes Earnings Assistance and Relief Tax Act (HEART).

### *Service Credit while on a Military Leave*

The Fund shall provide pensionable service credit for military service performed while an active firefighter for all periods after September 11, 2001, in which the firefighter made the required contributions corresponding to all or any portion of their military service time for calculation of future retirement benefits in accordance with the provisions of 40 ILCS 5/6-209. Participants will receive applicable service credits only for that portion of military time for which contributions are fully paid prior to application for retirement.

The contributions required for the purchase of these service credits are based on the full salary associated with the rank and grade held during this period of military service. If, during this period of military service, all or any portion of a member's full salary above the military pay that was received, that portion of the required contributions has already been made. However, the member is required to pay for the remaining balance of the contributions required on the full salary.

In December 2004, the Department of Labor issued final regulations *USERRA*. This Act provides that certain veterans are not required to pay interest on employee contributions attributable to periods in which they served in the military, provided that the contributions are paid within a prescribed period of time. Interest for in-service military time will begin to accrue on the earlier of (1) 5 years after returning to active duty or (2) 3 times the length of time they were away.

If the pension contributions associated with these available service credits is not paid, the periods served in the military will not be counted toward overall service for pension purposes. A refund of the partial contributions made during these periods would be issued at the time of your retirement.

***Death or Disability while on a Military Leave***

The Fund shall comply with all the requirements of the HEART Act for members who die or become disabled while serving in the military.

## ADDITIONAL INFORMATION

The full Summary of Benefits, including *Frequently Asked Questions* and contact information, is available at fabf.org.

## WHAT NEXT?

Your pension plan's website, fabf.org, has excellent on-line information for active and retired participants. You can also gain access to the plan's financial information. The audit and actuarial reports are a little tough to digest but are worth the effort for you to learn about your pension fund. Also, the actuarial report has an excellent summary of benefits that you can use to supplement your pension knowledge.

Contact the Chicago Fire fund's professional staff or the Trustees to assist you with any questions. Also, the pension fund staff and trustees present pre-retirement seminars for active members who are approaching retirement. Check with the office regarding the schedule and your eligibility to attend.

The website for IAFF Local 2 has Fraternal Order of Police Lodge 7 has information on retirement and medical insurance. See IAFF2.org.

As a Chicago firefighter or paramedic, you are not covered under Social Security for your police work. However, you may have earned Social Security benefits from work outside of fire/EMS. Be sure to read the section of this book on Social Security benefits.

Also, you are eligible to voluntarily save and invest a portion of your salary under the City's Section 457 Deferred Compensation Plan. Read the section of this book on deferred compensation and contact your plan at 1-877-677-3678 for specific information.

# 3

# SOCIAL SECURITY FOR CHICAGO POLICE AND FIRE

UP UNTIL RIGHT NOW, 2025, there were provisions of the Social Security Act that reduced benefits for retirees who had pensions from work outside of Social Security. These two provisions, the Windfall Elimination Provision (WEP) and the Government Pension Offset (GPO) were repealed in early 2025 by an act of Congress and signature by the President. The law, the *Social Security Fairness Act*, is retroactive to December 2023. So as you read this book, the same Social Security laws and formulas now apply to you as they do to every other worker in the country.

In previous editions of this book and in other training material, IPPFA provided a detailed explanation of the WEP and the GPO. This is no longer necessary and they are not addressed in this chapter, other than to emphasize their repeal. Instead, we now provide a basic overview of Social Security and instructions on where to go for more detailed information.

During the discussion, this chapter alternatively uses the familiar "SSA" for Social Security, as in Social Security Act or Social Security Administration.

## WHAT'S UP WITH SOCIAL SECURITY IN ILLINOIS?

Most Illinois sworn personnel do not participate in Social Security for their public safety work. Chicago employees, most suburban and downstate police and fire, the State University police and, Cook County all do not participate in Social Security. But most of these people will earn a Social Security check from their non-sworn work before, during (part-time), and after their police and fire careers. The monthly check that these workers will receive from Social

Security will be lower than the benefits paid to typical civilian employees. This is because these cops and firefighters spend twenty-plus years of their peak earning time outside of the Social Security system.

## WHY ARE MOST ILLINOIS FIRE AND POLICE OUTSIDE OF SOCIAL SECURITY?

Pretend that you could travel back to 1787 Philadelphia. You would observe thirteen guys sitting around a table at Independence Hall banging out a draft of what would become the US Constitution. A big issue then was the relationship between the federal and state governments. Nobody wanted the federal level to be superior. After the debate was over, the national government was given some express and strongly implied powers, and the rest were left to the states explicitly or generally under the 10th Amendment.

It seems kind of quaint and outdated now, given that the national government can use highway money to get the states to change speed limits. But this concept of *federalism* is still a guiding principle of our country; the national government and the states are both sovereign and draw their powers from a constitution. Affairs within a state are generally left to the state.

Does this have anything to do with the fact that Chicago fire and police don't pay into Social Security? Actually, yes. When SSA was established, state and local government employees were excluded from participating due to concerns about constitutionality. The employer-employee relationship was considered to be purely a state affair (and thus beyond the role of the national government). Also, the employer "match" under FICA was seen as a tax on one level of government by another.

In time, constitutional concerns abated and amendments to SSA allowed the states to participate if the employee group was not covered by a stand-alone retirement system. Eventually each of the fifty states entered into agreements with the Social Security Administration that defined who would or would not be covered by Social Security.

In Illinois, Chicago employees were excluded from SSA participation, along with the Article 3 and 4 police/fire systems (so-called "Downstate"), the state university public safety workers, and Cook County. Departments in small towns under 5,000 in population who participated in the Illinois Municipal Retirement Fund (IMRF) were placed in Social Security. Some of those small towns eventually became big towns, established their own police or fire fund, and left the IMRF. But they maintained their participation in Social Security as part of that deal. Other communities entered into something called a 218 agreement to participate in Social Security for all employees.

## THREE COPS WALK INTO A BAR...

After a regional training program, three police officers stop for a cold one to let traffic clear. One officer is from Chicago. He is covered by an Illinois Article 5 Chicago police pension and is not in Social Security for his police work. One cop is from Bartlett. He is in an Article 3 pension coverage but is *in* Social Security. The reason is that when the 1950's deal was cut with SSA, Bartlett was a small town protected by a few officers. They were too small to have established a police pension system so they were put in Social Security. But today it's a full-blown city with a police pension fund. Because of the Illinois/SSA deal, he and his coworkers are *in* Social Security forever. The third officer is from Bedford Park. She is in IMRF due to the population of that community and is also *in* Social Security.

What's the point of this bar story? History has created circumstances where the municipal police and fire responding to the same mutual aid disaster may have different pension plans or Social Security participation. A little odd, but true.

## SOCIAL SECURITY BASICS

Social Security was established in 1935 as part of the New Deal legislation following the Great Depression. By 2023, it was paying just over $1.4 trillion in annual benefits; the largest program in the federal budget. The system provides base-level retirement, disability, and survivor benefits to most American workers. It is sometimes referred to as a social insurance program, intended to keep people above the poverty level. Social Security is funded by employee contributions from the paycheck, an employer match of the same amount, and taxation on Social Security benefits. The long-term projections for funding of the system show a need for improvement either in revenue (higher taxes), a larger contribution base, benefit modifications, or some combination of the three. Private, individual-accounts as a future for Social Security have been discussed but not received favorably.

In the future, even if the Social Security trust fund balance drops to zero, worker and employer contributions and taxes would cover approximately 79% of future benefits. This is certainly a gap that America can manage. It's not productive for people to proclaim that *"Social Security is not going to be there for me."* It will be.

## The Basics—Who Pays for Social Security?

Workers pay 6.2% of their covered earnings for Social Security benefits and 1.45% for Medicare. Their employer matches those same payments. Wages over a certain level ($176,100 in 2025) are not taxed but are also not included in any benefit calculation. All workers, including those not in SSA, pay the 1.45% Medicare tax if they were hired after March 21, 1986. Virtually all Illinois fire and police are paying for Medicare and will be entitled to that retiree medical benefit when they turn 65.

You've seen the Social Security deduction taken out of your paycheck when you worked in SSA covered employment. It appears under the heading "FICA." This stands for Federal Insurance Contribution Act, the part of the Social Security legislation that sanctions the payroll deductions.

## The Basics—How Does Someone Earn a Benefit?

You are eligible for a Social Security benefit after you earn forty "credits" in the system. A credit is earned by receiving a certain amount of Social Security covered wages in a year. In 2025, the amount was $1,810 for one credit (it was lower in the past, will be higher in the future). Up to four credits can be earned in one year, so the requirement is sometimes called "forty quarters" as opposed to "forty credits." Forty quarters is almost 100% accurate, but a school teacher on a summer break could make a little over $7,200 and earn four credits during a single calendar quarter.

Two general truths result from this. First, it takes ten years of elapsed time in Social Security to earn a benefit. Second, it's not that hard to qualify for at least a small benefit. Even if you are out of SSA for thirty years in law enforcement or fire protection, there is still time before, during and after that to earn a small amount of SSA-covered wages and get your forty quarters/credits. Most people in Illinois public safety are entitled to or are on track to be entitled to Social Security benefits. You can tell if you have earned a benefit if you received a statement from Social Security telling you so. These statements are sent to participants at age 60 but are available online before and after that age if you have registered a personal "my Social Security" account at ssa.gov.

## The Basics—What Benefits are Earned?

Social Security benefits are paid to recipients, generally, in one of four forms:

- *Retirement* benefits from a worker's own record of Social Security earnings
- *Spousal* benefits from a spouse's record while the spouse is still alive
- *Survivor* benefits from a spouse's record after the spouse has died
- *Disability* benefits if you can no longer work due to illness or injury

It is important to note that a recipient may only receive one type of benefit at any one point in time. A person who receives a Survivor benefit gives up his or her own retirement benefit. A public pension fund does not work this way. If a married couple are both retired as Article 5 Chicago police retirees, when one dies the survivor may receive a survivor pension as well as her own retirement pension.

## BEYOND THE BASICS—RETIREMENT BENEFITS FROM YOUR OWN EARNINGS RECORD

Let's look first at how Social Security retirement benefits are calculated using the worker's own record of earnings under Social Security. This is the way that most Social Security benefits are paid, as opposed to disability, spousal and survivor benefits.

### Replacement Rates, Final Salary, and Social Security

Remember your police or fire pension formula. Your benefit is calculated based on the salary at the end of your career, which is then multiplied by a percentage factor based on your years of work. This percentage is called the "replacement rate" (*i.e.*, the portion of your salary that is replaced by your pension). So 75% of final pay for thirty years of service, 50% for twenty years of service, or 65% for line-of-duty disability reflect replacement rates of 75%, 50%, and 65% respectively multiplied by final pay.

Social Security uses the same concept with two fairly major deviations. The first difference is how the salary for the computation is determined. The second is that varying replacement rates are used on different portions of your earnings. It's a bit complicated, but understandable.

### Salary Used for Social Security Calculation

In the Chicago public safety pension systems, the salary used for the Tier 1 pension calculation is the average salary over the final four years of employment. In Social Security, it is the highest 35 years; *almost the entire working life of a person.* But, because some of those wages were earned so long ago, the Social Security formula adjusts (*i.e.*, indexes) those wages to inflation. Thus, if a person who retired in 2024 earned $10,000 back in 1989, Social Security indexes those wages forward to $26,916 when they calculate the person's average indexed earnings over his or her 35-year total.

A notable truth, especially for fire and police personnel: calendar years with no SSA earnings ($0) count when calculating the average earnings. Consequently, if a worker had inflation adjusted earnings of $15,000 yearly for five years, then no Social Security earnings during a 30-year public safety career ($0), then $50,000 annually for ten years, his or her average indexed earnings over the highest 35 years would be as follows:

| | |
|---|---|
| 10 years at $50,000 | $500,000 |
| 5 years at $15,000 | $75,000 |
| 20 years at $0 | $0 |
| Total—Highest 35 Years | $575,000 |
| Average over 35 Years | $16,430 |
| Indexed Monthly Average – 35 yrs | $1,369 |

### *Replacement Rates*

After the average salary is calculated (called "average indexed monthly earnings" or AIME), the SSA system then uses different replacement rates for up to three separate levels of an individual retiree's indexed income. For persons attaining age 62 in 2025, those income levels and replacement rates are:

| | |
|---|---|
| First $1,226 in monthly earnings | **90%*** |
| Next $6,165 in monthly earnings | 32% |
| Over $7,391 to taxable maximum | 15% |

Let's look at an example of how these rates work for three different Social Security recipients:

| Monthly Average Wage | Calculation | Benefit | Replacement Rate |
|---|---|---|---|
| ***Retiree #1***—$800 | $800 @ 90% | $720 | 90%* |
| ***Retiree #2***—$1,600 | $1,226 @ 90%<br>$374 @ 32% | $1,223 | 76% |
| ***Retiree #3***—$8,500 | $1,226 @ 90%<br>$6,165 @ 32%<br>$1,109 @ 15% | $3,242 | 38% |

*This percentage was 40% under the repealed WEP.

Notice the progressive nature of Social Security benefits (lower income earnings receive a higher percentage replacement). The very low paid worker gets 90% of pay in Social Security benefit. The highest paid worker shown gets some at 90%, most at 32%, and a portion at 15%. The highest wage earner's final replacement rate is 38%. That 38% doesn't appear anywhere in the published formulas—it's a weighted compilation of the three different published rates of 90, 32, and 15 percent.

### Estimating Your Own Benefit

What does this mean for a Chicago firefighter or police officer? Your earning in Social Security covered employment will likely be somewhat sparse, and your benefit will be lower than your private-sector friends and relatives. Using the example of a person with lifetime index earnings of $1,369 shown on page 46, the Social Security benefit amounts to $1,149 at the Full Retirement Age (more on the FRA later). If you earned higher average earnings during your working life in Social Security, your benefits will be higher. Earn less than that amount, the benefit will be lower.

A superior approach is for everyone to go to the *ssa.gov* website and register for an account for access to their own private information. Once you have registered, you can examine your own record and run projections based on your earnings to-date and your estimated Social Security earnings in the future.

The good news is that since the Windfall Elimination Provision (WEP) has now been repealed, your benefit will be higher and the opportunity to estimate your own Social Security benefits is the same as every other worker. Previously it was necessary to download your earnings record from ssa.gov and then input the data into a special WEP Calculator. That is no longer needed.

## SOCIAL SECURITY BENEFITS FROM YOUR LIVING SPOUSE'S RECORD

In general, a retiree receives Social Security benefits equal to (a) the benefits earned from his own work record or (b) one-half of his spouse's Social Security benefit, whichever is higher. Two examples follow:

| | |
|---|---|
| Mark's SSA Benefit | $2,000 |
| Sue's SSA Benefit from her own record | $800 |

Sue will receive the following:

| | |
|---|---|
| From her own record | $800 |
| From Mark's Record | $200 |
| **Sue's Total Benefit** | **$1,000** |

Sue is entitled to her own SSA benefit plus a spouse's benefit so that her total Social Security payment is one-half of Mark's. Together, the couple will receive $3,000 (Sue's share does not come out of Mark's benefit). A second example:

| | |
|---|---|
| Ward's Benefit | $2,200 |
| June's SSA Benefit from her own record | $0 |

June will receive the following:

| | |
|---|---|
| From her own record | $0 |
| From Ward's Record | $1,100 |
| **June's Total Benefit** | **$1,100** |

June was at home taking care of her two sons and never worked enough time in SSA covered employment to accumulate forty credits, so she has no benefit on her own record. But she is still entitled to benefits from Ward's record of earnings. Together the couple will receive $3,300.

## The Government Pension Offset (GPO)—REPEALED

Previously, the Government Pension Offset provided for a reduction in Social Security benefits *from a spouse's record* of 66-cents for every dollar a City of Chicago employee received from a state or municipal pension if he or she was not in Social Security at the police or fire department. At the time, examples weren't really needed since the GPO usually eliminated any benefit payable under a living spouse's record.

But, as noted, the GPO has now been repealed. A Chicago police officer of firefighter may receive an unreduced Spousal benefit if his or her own earned benefit is less than one-half of the spouse's Social Security benefit.

### Is a Spousal Benefit Helpful for a Chicago Police Officer or Firefighter?

The advantages of the now unrestricted Spousal benefit will vary among Illinois first-responders. For the fire and police outside of Chicago who may be Social Security at their public safety job, there is no advantage. Their own Social Security benefit will be higher than one-half of a spouse's, even if she or he was a tech executive and paid the maximum in Social Security taxes.

For City of Chicago workers who are outside of Social Security for most of their careers, there may or may not be an advantage. If your spouse was a full-time parent for many years and earned only a modest Social Security benefit on her earnings, your own benefit may be more than one-half of hers (even though you were outside the Social Security system for decades). This would leave no Spousal benefit available for you.

However, if your spouse worked mostly full-time in Social Security covered employment, one-half of his or her benefit may be a little more, somewhat more or *much* more than your own Social Security. Under those circumstances, a Spousal benefit will be advantageous for you. The good news is that the Social Security application processes examines both benefits, your own and any Spousal benefit, that you may be entitled to.

## SOCIAL SECURITY BENEFITS AS A SURVIVING SPOUSE

In retirement, a surviving spouse can collect up to 100% of the late spouse's Social Security benefit. There are also Survivor benefits available prior to retirement, with age and/or dependent child rules that apply. About 3.8 million widows and widowers were receiving Survivor benefits as of August 2024 (source: AARP).

However, in retirement, a surviving spouse gives up his or her own Social Security benefit once a Survivor benefit is paid. This is different than a public pension system. If a married couple consists of two retired Chicago police officers, when one dies the other can continue the retirement pension and be paid the 50% survivor benefit from the CPD pension plan. Not so with Social Security.

Previously, just like the Spousal benefit, the Government Pension Offset provided for a reduction in Social Security *Survivor* benefits. This rule no longer applies. It is now more likely that an Illinois police or fire professional will receive a Social Security Survivor benefit than before, but is not guaranteed. Remember that if your own Social Security benefit is higher than your wife or husband's, no Survivor benefit will be paid to you because your own benefit is higher.

## A WORD ABOUT DIVORCE

Both Spousal and Survivor benefits are available based on the earnings record of an ex-spouse as long as the marriage lasted 10 years and the recipient remains unmarried. This is a special circumstance and should be personally explored if it may affect you. However, at the time of retirement, the Social Security application process should bring this opportunity into the calculation of a Spousal or Survivor benefit.

## A WORD ABOUT DISABILITY BENEFITS

In addition to retirement and survivor benefits, Social Security also provides disability benefits. However, the definition of disability under Social Security is harder to meet than the definition under the Illinois Article 5-6 police or fire pension system. This is appropriate. A firefighter who can't throw a ladder or a police officer who can't run after a fleeing suspect is disabled from public safety work and should receive a pension. But if that same person has the education, skills and abilities to perform other, non-physical work, then Social Security might not consider them to be disabled. So disability benefits from Social Security are not a sure thing even if your local pension board finds you disabled under the Chicago fire or police pension codes.

In addition to meeting the Social Security definition of disabled, a worker must have had Social Security covered wages within a timeframe established by Social Security in order to receive disability benefits. If you qualify, the SSA benefit will be fairly small since your earnings exclude your professional wages. Still, that small monthly disability check could still provide a person with critical income at a time when it is sorely needed.

## SOME WORDS ABOUT CLAIMING STRATEGIES

Whether or not you are in or out of Social Security for your public safety job, all of us will be faced with decisions regarding when and how to receive our Social Security benefit. There is a fancy phrase for this—a claiming strategy. This concept has been touched on in previous editions of this book. It was always an important subject, but with the repeal of the Government Pension Offset, there are now more claiming possibilities for Illinois fire and police personnel.

At the simple end of the spectrum is the issue of what age to begin taking the benefit. A retiree can begin as early as age 62 (with some limits on allowable wage income) or may defer as late as age 70. With each month of delay, the benefit goes up. A retiree and spouse might make different decisions on the age at which to draw SSA benefits. In this approach, some income starts to flow into the household but some is deferred to a later age (with the money growing each year it is deferred).

The information that follows touches on some of the basic information needed to develop a claiming strategy. Neither IPPFA nor the authors are experts in this subject, and advice on how to access the necessary expertise will follow.

### Full Retirement Age (FRA)

The FRA is the age at which the calculated benefit (shown in the prior charts and examples) is payable to the retiree. In Social Security parlance this is called the Primary Insurance Amount (PIA). Your Full Retirement Age is shown on the following chart:

| YEAR BORN | FULL RETIREMENT AGE |
|---|---:|
| Thru 1954 | 66 years old, 0 months |
| 1955 | 66 years old, 2 months |
| 1956 | 66 years old, 4 months |
| 1957 | 66 years old, 6 months |
| 1958 | 66 years old, 8 months |
| 1959 | 66 years old, 10 months |
| 1960 and later | 67 years old |

## Claiming Before your Full Retirement Age

You can claim your Social Security benefit as early as age 62. If you claim before your Full Retirement Age, the benefit is reduced each month that you draw before your FRA. Examples of the reduction amount based on an FRA of 67 years old follow:

| CLAIMING AGE | REDUCTION |
|---|---|
| 62 | 30.0% |
| 63 | 24.9% |
| 64 | 20.0% |
| 65 | 13.1% |
| 66 | 6.7% |

In addition to experiencing a reduction in the monthly payment, persons who draw their Social Security before their Full Retirement Age are subject to an annual limit on wages and self-employment income. If the retiree exceeds the limit, their Social Security is reduced in a following year by 50-cents for every $1 that the limit was exceeded. In 2025 that annual wage limit is $23,400. This is an indexed amount so it will be higher in years after 2025. Note that the income limit is higher in the calendar year that you actually reach the FRA.

## Deferring Social Security

You may also defer your retirement benefit after your Full Retirement Age. If you do so, your benefit goes up each month by a uniform increase of 8% per year (prorated monthly). Examples based on an FRA of 67 follow:

| CLAIMING AGE | INCREASE IN SOCIAL SECURITY |
|---|---|
| 67 | Calculated Benefit |
| 68 | 8% higher |
| 69 | 16% higher |
| 70 | 24% higher |
| 71 and above | No further increases |

## What's the Best Age to Draw?

Whether there is a "best age" or not is subject to debate. There is a lot of material written and easily available on this subject. Overall, delaying your Social Security makes sense if you are going to live longer than the average American. You will receive the higher amount for more months and years.

Generally, the formulas are "neutral" based on system-wide life expectancy. Under such neutrality, if Maddie draws at 62, Mike at 67 and Mandy at 70, they all are making a good decision if it fits their needs.

While the formulas are based on system-wide life expectancy, public employees generally have educations levels at high school or above, middle class incomes and health insurance while they are working. These are all drivers of increased life expectancy. And while police and fire are identified as individuals whose life expectancy may be shorter than others due to the physical and other stresses of the job, that is only when compared to persons in similar economic positions. Also, first-responders have passed a fairly thorough medical examination and a very arduous physical fitness test. In short, your life expectancy is likely better than that reflected in the Social Security calculations.

Also, the reduction formulas do not take gender into account. Since women live longer than men, women should consider delaying their Social Security.

One approach can be, if you need the money, then begin taking Social Security. If you don't need it, delay so that your benefit is higher in your later years and any potential Survivor benefit you leave to a spouse will be higher.

## Other Claiming Considerations

There may be the opportunity for some married couples to coordinate their Social Security claiming to their advantage. One spouse can begin drawing on their own benefit and then later switch to a Spousal benefit when their spouse retires.

A more complicated issue involves a retiree applying for his or her benefit but then suspending immediate receipt. This was allowed previously, but a new law quashed this benefit claiming opportunity for anyone who wasn't

62 by January 2nd of 2016. When it was allowed, the approach permitted the spouse to begin collecting a Spousal benefit off of the retiree's record. Later, that spouse could switch to benefits under his or her own SSA record, which would have grown each year the benefit was deferred up until age 70. For Illinois sworn personnel who are in Social Security, "file and suspend" could have presented some very nice alternatives. But the opportunity is now gone for most retirees.

Serious consideration of claiming strategies is beyond the scope of this book. There is a lot written on this subject, available free online. You can also engage the services of an expert, in person or online, to run specific strategies based on your (and your spouse's) actual Social Security record. You could spend a few hundred dollars at most, but be guided to a strategy worth more than $100,000 over a couple's lifetimes.

Two services that have been examined by the authors are listed below. IPPFA does not endorse any provider, but these services appeared to be thorough and reasonable in cost. They are:

**MaximizemySocialSecurity.com**

This is the website of a Boston University professor and author on benefit maximization. It is recommended by Terry Savage, a nationally syndicated columnist.

**SocialSecurityAdvisors.com**

They provide a very complete report as well as an option to speak to an expert.

Also, if you have a personal financial advisor, that individual may have advanced software that can assist you in making a claiming decision.

## SOCIAL SECURITY WRAP UP

### Chapter Summary

There is a lot of information in the chapter you just read. Let's summarize where we have traveled:

Social Security benefits are based on a worker's wages over his or her working life, essentially 35 years. Forty credits (usually ten years) must be earned to obtain any benefit.

City of Chicago employees are not covered by Social Security while in City employment. Still, they are likely to earn Social Security benefits from work before, during, and after their public safety careers. They will generally earn a lower benefit than their civilian counterparts because of the many high-wage years they spend outside of Social Security.

Prior to 2025, special rules applied to the benefit calculation of persons who earned pensions outside of Social Security covered employment. Those rules, the Windfall Elimination Provision (WEP) and the Government Pension Offset (GPO) were repealed upon adoption of the *Social Security Fairness Act.* Because of this change, there is a higher likelihood that Illinois first-responders will earn benefits under the Spousal and Survivor benefit allowances.

The "three-legged stool" of retirement income includes pension, Social Security, and personal savings. For most Illinois fire and police, the Social Security leg will be lessened by a career outside of Social Security. Their generally higher pension benefits than the civilian workforce are designed in part to make up for this lower Social Security benefit.

### Is Social Security Participation Valuable?

Yes. There is almost always a benefit to earning Social Security covered wages. If a job opportunity presents itself, either part-time or after your police/fire retirement, there is no reason not to pay the 6.2% payroll deduction and qualify for or earn a higher monthly benefit.

This applies across the board. For a new public safety professional who only has a few years in Social Security before taking the oath, it will pay in the long run for him or her to gain forty (40) credits/quarters and qualify. For someone who has already achieved Social Security eligibility and is retiring from the police or fire department, adding to their Social Security record prior to attaining age 62 or even later will add to their retirement income.

And, as discussed above, active employment in Social Security can qualify a person or increase benefits should he or she become disabled.

## SOCIAL SECURITY PUBLICATIONS

Social Security has numerous publications available for download (or audio listening) from their website, ssa.gov. A few publications that may help in providing an overall view of Social Security are listed below. Some of these publications need to be updated to remove any reference to the WEP and the GPO. If you run across these provisions, don't worry about them. Recommended publications are:

***Understanding the Benefits***
Publication #05-10024, January 2024
Get an overview of all Social Security programs and Medicare.

***Retirement Benefits***
05-10035, January 2024
Learn about Social Security retirement benefits: how you earn coverage; how to apply; how benefits are figured; and how to decide when to retire.

***Your Retirement Benefit: How It is Figured***
05-10070, January 2023
Learn about the formula used to calculate Social Security retirement benefits and take advantage of a worksheet to help you estimate your retirement benefits.

***Disability Benefits***
05-10029, March 2024
People with disabilities can get basic information on Social Security benefits.

## ANYTHING ELSE?

Again, you should consider opening up an account with Social Security (ssa.gov) to at least view a statement of earnings and benefits estimates or go further to see your entire record and run your own estimates.

When you get to retirement, become your own expert on the issue of claiming strategies or find a professional online or in person to assist you.

As the Social Security Administration works to implement the *Social Security Fairness Act* (and the elimination of the WEP and GPO), persons already receiving Social Security benefits will have a heightened interest in SSA's progress on these changes.

For those of you who are not yet collecting Social Security, their systems should be able to accurately handle your application when you apply in the future.

For those of you who are already collecting, the *Act* is retroactive to December 2023. It will take time for the Social Security Administration to re-calculate your benefits and make retroactive payments. At the date of this publication, Social Security had the following information on their website. This website, www.ssa.gov/benefits/retirement/social-security-fairness-act.html, will be updated from time to time.

> ***If you have previously filed for Social Security benefits and they are partially or completely offset,*** at this time, you do not need to take any action except to verify that the Social Security Administration has your current mailing address and direct deposit information if it has recently changed. Most people can do this online by accessing their personal Social Security account without calling or visiting a Social Security office.
>
> ***If you have not previously filed for Social Security benefits,*** you are receiving a public pension and you are interested in filing for benefits, you can file for benefits online at ssa.gov or schedule an appointment.

Most retired Chicago and other Illinois fire/police who are age-eligible for Social Security benefits have applied for and are receiving benefits. However, there will be some public employees who never applied for benefits because they did not have forty credits and their pension would have totally offset any Spousal benefit. Social Security is now recommending that they apply for benefits.

We will be watching for information from Social Security as well as the websites of organizations which have closely followed these changes. Specifically, the Illinois Retired Teachers Association (irtaonline.org) and the Texas Retired Teachers Association (trta.org) are likely to have as up-to-date information as is available. IPPFA will send out bulletins when there is news worth sharing.

Finally, good luck on making the most of your Social Security benefits upon the passage of the *Social Security Fairness Act.*

# 4

# PUBLIC EMPLOYEE DEFERRED COMPENSATION

## WHAT IS DEFERRED COMPENSATION?

When a person receives wages (*i.e.*, compensation), income taxes are withheld, and the amount earned is reported to the IRS at the end of the year.

However, sections of the Internal Revenue Code (IRC) and Illinois law allow an employee to *defer* receipt of some wages on a pre-tax basis until after he or she retires. At the time these deferred wages are earned, they are neither received in the paycheck, subjected to tax withholding, nor reported as taxable to the IRS (unless a Roth option is chosen, which is explained later). The money instead is deposited into an account and invested as directed by the employee. When the accumulated dollars are ultimately received after retirement (or sooner in some cases), the withdrawal payments are then reported to the IRS as taxable distributions. This deferral of wages and taxes until after retirement is commonly referred to as deferred compensation or "deferred comp."

For most public employees, deferred compensation under IRC code Section 457 is the strongest part of the "personal savings" leg of the three-legged retirement income stool (pension, Social Security and personal savings). Your personal savings can of course include the value of your home, brokerage accounts, individual retirement accounts, investment real estate, and bank savings. But the ability to save through the paycheck on a tax-advantaged basis has made deferred compensation a large personal asset for many public employees. For this reason, and because your deferred compensation operates a little differently than your neighbor's 401(k) plan or your nurse-sister's 403(b), Section 457 savings is the focal point of the chapter of personal savings for Chicago fire and police.

## Chapter Outline

In this chapter, we will first look at some background information on Section 457 plans. Then, we'll "follow the money." We cover how money is put into the plan, how it is invested along the way, and how it is withdrawn to meet your goal of a secure retirement. Regarding the middle part, this is not an investment guide. There is really nothing unique about 457 investing when compared to other supplemental plans where the employee self-directs the account. But we'll still go over the basics. Then the chapter ends with hopefully good tips for you on how to proceed, along with some final enthusiasm for these excellent plans.

## Legal Standing

Deferred compensation systems have evolved under legislation and IRS rulings specifically in relation to the employer of each worker. Each plan is designated by the section of the Internal Revenue Code that authorizes and governs the deferral. Section 401(k) plans, the most prominent type of deferred compensation, grew out of profit-sharing plans and have been primarily used by private sector employees in for-profit companies. Section 403(b) has been the primary plan for employees of education, scientific, and charitable organizations. These plans are found in many not-for-profit hospitals, and both public and private schools. Finally, **Section 457** plans are available to employees of state and local government and, in a modified form, to some management and professional employees of not-for-profit agencies. We'll concentrate on the government form available to City of Chicago employees.

## HISTORY OF 457 PLANS

Prior to 1978, various organizations obtained "private letter rulings" from the IRS allowing public employees to defer compensation. An actual code section authorizing deferrals was subsequently included in the *Revenue Act of 1978* as a new Section 457(b) of the code. There have been revisions since then, the notable being the improvements in the 1996, 2000, and 2002 reform laws. Most importantly, the 1996 reform law established that funds held in a 457 plan are in a trust fund and are not available to the municipalities' general creditors. This change, long overdue, followed the bankruptcy of Orange County (California) after an investment scandal.

Changes in 2000 and 2002 went a long way in making the 457 plan look more like its private sector cohorts under 401(k) and 403(b). The allowable contribution amounts were made to be very similar between the plans. The withdrawal rules and the opportunity for rollover from one plan to the other or to an Individual Retirement Account (IRA) were made similar. Prior to these reforms, it was very important for public sector employees to be given special instruction on 457 plan deferred compensation (the withdrawal rules were particularly complicated). That need has lessened now—public employees can obtain general information from the financial industry or media on deferred compensation and then check with their plan administrator for specific 457 plan rules.

Chicago has offered a deferred compensation plan for decades. The plan is administered by Nationwide Retirement Solutions (NRS). Specific information on the plan and various forms are available at chicagodeferredcomp.com.

## HOW DOES TAX DEFERRAL IMPROVE RETIREMENT SAVINGS?

In a traditional tax-deferred plan, an employee elects to defer compensation at a set amount or a percentage of pay. When he or she is paid each payday, the deferred compensation amount is deducted from the paycheck and deposited into a special account. Taxes withheld from the paycheck are calculated on the basis that the amount deferred was taken from the paycheck "before taxes." So, the paycheck does not go down as much as the total amount put into the deferred compensation account. Then, at the end of the year, the amount deferred is not reported to the IRS or state as a taxable wage. An example follows.

### *A Tale of Two Savers*

To see how pre-tax deferring compensation compares to savings through taxable channels, let's look at two savers, Tim and Suzanne. They both earn $4,000 monthly and can afford to put away $300 per month for retirement savings. Tim opens a brokerage account for his investments and has his employer sends the $300 to his account via the ACH automated banking system. Suzanne joins her public employer's deferred compensation plan. Here's how their monthly gross and take-home pay are affected (excluding Social Security or pension contributions, which are unchanged by either approach).

| | TIM | SUZANNE |
|---|---|---|
| Salary | $4,000 | $4,000 |
| Deferred Compensation | 0 | (428) |
| Taxable Wages | $4,000 | $3,572 |
| Federal Tax | 540 | 427 |
| State Tax | 200 | 185 |
| Brokerage Account Deposit | 300 | 0 |
| Net Pay | $2,960 | $2,960 |

Tim and Suzanne both have the same monthly net pay but Suzanne saves $428 monthly while Tim puts away only $300. This happens because Suzanne's tax deferral advantage on the $428 deposit reduces her net pay by only the $300 that she can afford. Of course, Tim is free and clear on the taxes for the principle amount he has saved; Suzanne eventually does pay the tax on her $428. But let's see how that works out.

Suppose Tim earns 7.5% annually on his savings and pays 23.1% in tax on his earnings each year. If he keeps up his savings/investment/tax program for 30 years, he'll have $281,200 in his account at retirement. If Suzanne earns the same 7.5% return over 30 years, her balance will accumulate to $551,000. She still owes tax on that amount, but she has almost twice the amount that Tim has. Tax rates are simply not high enough to take away the advantages she has already gained.

Also, there are other factors in her favor. First, if she lives in a state that doesn't tax 457 withdrawals, such as Illinois, she will avoid the state tax completely. Moreover, if she draws her money out gradually (while still experiencing investment earnings), she will continue to enjoy the benefit of tax deferral while drawing money out at levels that do not trigger excessive taxes.

Personal financial experts are virtually unanimous in their advice that deferred compensation is an excellent way to save. Even changes in the tax code, which reduced taxes for people who own stocks and mutual funds outside of deferred compensation, have not diminished the attractiveness of these plans.

## NOTE

If an employee routinely pays a large amount of money to the IRS at year-end, enrolling in or increasing deferrals In a Section 457 plan may not eliminate a large tax payment on April 15th, although it will reduce it somewhat. The employee may still need to adjust his tax or her withholding by completing a revised declaration of exemptions (W-4), which is available from the payroll office.

## WHAT ABOUT THE ROTH APPROACH?

There was a senator from Delaware named Roth who in 1997 got Congress to establish the Roth IRA. In time, that morphed over into a Roth 401(k) and eventually a Roth 457 option. Your employer, the City of Chicago, does offer a Roth 457 option.

Most public employees save for retirement using a traditional tax-deferred 457 plan as opposed to a Roth. Because of that, we've concentrated this chapter of the book on the method that most of us have used. Also, the pros and cons of Roth savings are the same for you as for your IRA or 401(k) saving friends and relatives. So, you can get good information from most sources that provide such advice.

But, in case this Roth thing is new to you, we provide just a short explanation. In a Roth 457 plan, there is no tax savings or other advantage at the time the employee makes his or her payroll deduction deposit. So if Suzanne in my example put $428 monthly into a Roth 457 plan, her pay would go down $428, not the $300 shown in the table. However, the money earned on Roth deposits is not taxed at the time of a qualified withdrawal. To be qualified, the withdrawal has to take place after age 59-1/2 and at least five years after the initial Roth contribution. If a withdrawal is taken before these two requirements are met, investment earnings would be subject to federal taxation (but not the principal amount deposited). So the earnings in a Roth account are not simply tax-deferred, they are *tax-exempt*—a superior tax treatment at the time of withdrawal.

To summarize, the Roth has no tax break at the time of the deposit, but *all* of the earnings are tax-exempt when qualified withdrawal rules are followed. Not just deferred, *exempt*. The traditional 457 approach gives the saver a tax break going in, essentially creating more money to be saved, but those tax-deferred deposits and all earnings are eventually taxed.

## RULES FOR DEFERRING INCOME

A maximum of $23,500 may be deferred in 2025, which will be indexed to inflation in the future. There is no statutory minimum amount of deferral.

There is a provision of Section 457 that allows an employee to exceed the annual maximum, up to double the amount of the annual maximum, in the last three years prior to being eligible to receive a pension from the employer-sponsored retirement plan. The additional amount deferred is limited to amounts that the employee *could* have legally deferred in the past but did not. It is further limited to the annual amount for regular contributions. For example, if the employee could have deferred $7,500 in each year of his first ten years of employment ($75,000) but only deferred $45,000 during those years, he or she has $30,000 left that can be deferred in the last three years prior to eligibility for receipt of pension (in addition to the regular maximum but nor more than twice the annual maximum in total).

This extra allowance is nicknamed "**the Catch-up Provision**," since the employee is catching-up on deferrals that could have been made earlier in his career.

The 2000 reform law added an additional savings opportunity, the so-called "Age 50 Catch-up Provision." This provision allowed a person over age 50 to contribute an additional $1,000 in 2002, incrementally increasing to $7,500 in 2025. This additional amount cannot be contributed in a year when the standard Catch-up Provision is being used. This Age 50 allowance is not dependent upon the existence of "unused deferrals" in prior years. It is simply additional authority to defer salary.

And now, under a new retirement law called SECURE 2.0, the IRS has announced an increased contribution limit in 2025 for those ages 60-63. This additional catchup rule allows someone who qualifies to contribute an additional $11,250 to the standard contribution limit of $23,500. Note that once participants turn 64, they revert to the standard Age 50+ catch-up contribution limit. And some good news, the amount of this SECURE 2.0 enhanced catch-up may increase in future years as it is indexed to the Age 50+ catch-up allowance.

## THE RULE OF 72

Catch-up provisions are okay. But, if you can afford to, it's so much better to put a little more money into deferred compensation during your career than a lot of money at the end. Let's explore that idea further and learn an important investment concept along the way.

The variables that affect how much you accumulate in deferred compensation are the amount you put in, your investment return, and how long the money stays on deposit. The time factor is huge. The longer the amount of time your money is on deposit, the more fantastic things happen to it.

There is a mathematical **Rule of 72**. An investor can take his or her expected rate of investment earnings and divide it into 72. The product of that division is the length of time in years that it will take the invested money to double in value. So, at an easy-to-use estimate of 7.2% annual investment return, money doubles every ten years (72 divided by 7.2% = 10 years). If $3,000 is invested, it will become $6,000 in ten years, $12,000 in twenty years and $24,000 in thirty years. If the rate of earnings is higher, say at 8%, money will then double every nine years, not ten. At thirty years the same deposits will have grown to not $24,000 but $30,000.

The Rule of 72 amplifies the importance of time. If a person made that same $3,000 investment three years earlier and had it on deposit for thirty-three years, the same one-time deposit of $3,000 at 8% will grow to $38,000—26% more than the same dollars invested for thirty years.

Remember Suzanne's accumulated $551,000. Say she increases her savings in the last three years by a total of $30,000 by "catching up" $10,000 each year. If she does this, her end-of-thirty-year total grows to $584,000. If she instead found a way to put in the additional $30,000 by saving $1,000 more in each of the thirty years of her participation, the balance at the end is $658,000. True story.

Time is your friend. Save as much as you reasonably can as early as you can. Capitalize on "The Rule of 72."

### BUT YOU MAY WANT TO CATCH-UP TO SAVE STATE TAXES

Although the Catch-up Provisions aren't hugely effective for long term savings, there is a short-term advantage: money withdrawn from Section 457 plans in Illinois is not subject to state taxes. So, a participant can save 4.95% on his or her money going into the plan (since it's not subject to Illinois withholding or reporting) but state taxes are not assessed on the money when it is withdrawn. Thus, state taxes are not just deferred, they are eliminated completely. This is true on all your deferred compensation deposits and earnings if you remain an Illinois taxpayer and the law is not changed.

## DEFERRED COMPENSATION— INVESTMENT OVERVIEW

This is an area in which you are not different. Any book, article or advice from an expert that educates you about asset allocation for retirement savings works for Section 457 plans.

Like the 401(k) plan, most Section 457 plans, including Chicago, offer a variety of investments in the form of either public mutual funds or commingled investment accounts managed by investment experts. A participant can select from fixed or guaranteed rate investment accounts, various stock accounts, government and/or corporate bond accounts, or blended or balanced accounts that offer a combination of stocks, bonds, and short-term investment instruments. Your investment is held in trust and can only be used for your benefit under the rules of the plan and the Internal Revenue Code.

Since you can get advice or information anywhere and your investment goals and selections are not any different than your neighbor with a 401(k) plan, this book is not an investment guide. But we'll go over the basics, plus you may well have a certain amount of financial acumen anyway. You can then decide how much more research or assistance you need, if any, on this aspect of your personal savings and retirement plan.

## WHO BELONGS IN WHAT INVESTMENT?

Professional investors break down the types of investments into broad asset classes—stocks, bonds, real estate, commodities, *etc*. How those are mixed together in a portfolio is called **asset allocation**. How does one select an asset allocation that is right for his or her long-term goals? You need to spend some time on this, as the experts say that asset allocation decision is far more important than which individual investments or funds that you select.

The American economic system rewards ownership. It is more advantageous to own a company than to lend the company (or a government) money, although lending certainly has its place in the economy and as an investment. When you invest in a stock mutual fund or other type of stock account, you are taking partial ownership of the many companies in the account. So, it is not a surprise that, by all historic measurements, stock market investments outperform other asset classes. Accordingly, the percentage of your asset allocation that you have in the stock market should be a key consideration.

The reality of investment returns supports the philosophical view of the benefits of ownership. Here are the various domestic market returns from January 1st, 1926 (before the Great Depression) to December 31, 2023:

| ASSET CLASS | ANNUAL RETURN |
|---|---|
| Small Company Stocks | 11.8% |
| Large Company Stocks | 10.3% |
| U.S. Government Bonds | 5.1% |
| 30-Day U.S. Treasury Bills | 3.3% |

***Source Ibbotson SBBI***

Of course, such returns and those in the future may come with great volatility. Just look at what we've experienced over the past two decades: fantastic highs, retractions, periods of steady returns, two huge drops, and then big recoveries. But if you are a long-term investor, the long-term returns in stocks beat the safer bets, as long as you make some effort to manage the volatility, such as disciplined rebalancing.

## PUBLIC EMPLOYEES ARE AGGRESSIVE INVESTORS

Both from the records of the IPPFA Benefits Division and anecdotally from other workers, we see that public employees tend to be fairly aggressive in their deferred compensation investing. That is, they have a relatively high percentage of their asset allocation in the stock market. They thus often capture more of the gains possible, *i.e.* those indicated in the preceding chart.

Whether these investors are less risk-adverse than the average investor or maybe just smarter, underlying this trend is a valid long-term saving concept. Because public employees are more likely to have a pension, *i.e.*, a guaranteed retirement income, they can take more risk with their separate, personal retirement savings.

## 100% MINUS YOUR AGE

If you prefer to be a little less aggressive, some personal financial experts suggest a basic formula known as **100% minus your age**. If you follow this formula, the percentage of your retirement assets that you will have in equities (*i.e.*, the stock market) will be equal to 100% minus your age. For example, if a person is 45 years old and subtracts his age from 100, the difference of 55 (*i.e.*, 55%) represents a suggested level for him to invest in stocks. If he was deferring $100 per paycheck, $55 would go to stocks and the balance would go to the bond or fixed accounts.

Using this formula, or a similar approach, a saver ends up investing more aggressively when he or she is younger. At age 22, "100% minus your age" puts 78% of money in stocks. Continuing, the formula reduces stock holdings as a person ages and ultimately approaches retirement. At age 60, only 40% of the money will be in stocks. This is what you may want to happen, because the amount of the portfolio that is in a volatile investment is reduced as retirement approaches. But you still maintain some opportunity for growth to beat inflation or a hopefully long life. Under this approach, even an octogenarian has 20% of her retirement account in the stock market.

## WHY NOT 100% IN STOCKS?

Here is another math lesson. If I have a $1,000 stock investment that drops 25%, what do I have left? The answer is $750. This isn't too hard to figure out. But here is an important follow up question. What investment return do I then need to get my $750 back to $1,000 before I can grow my initial investment even by one penny? The answer is 33%, not the 25% I originally lost. Volatility is not just your investment going up and down—*volatility can hurt your returns.* That's why a 100% allocation to stock may be a little too risky.

Also, when the market is down for a prolonged period, your fixed income investments will help you keep your balances up *and* reinforce your confidence in deferred compensation. Further, placing a small portion of a portfolio in another asset class, even one that does not perform as well as your core investments, can result in less volatility and higher earnings if the account is rebalanced from time to time (more on that to follow).

Both of these factors are where the phase **diversification** comes in; you've heard that before. A variety of asset classes in your diversified portfolio keeps you almost whole when one asset class underperforms. You also can rebalance between the asset classes to your long-term benefit.

## REBALANCING

Very importantly, an allocation to both stocks and fixed income which you regularly rebalance will give you the opportunity to actually "buy low, sell high" for a long-term overall gain.

Let's say firefighter Addie is an avid deferred compensation investor and currently deposits her money each payday along a 60/40 stock/bond mix, with some of the stock piece in small companies and foreign stocks, and some of the fixed income piece to the plan's stable value fund. Over time, thanks to the pretty good performance in all aspects of her stock allocation, her account balance looks like this:

| | | |
|---|---|---|
| Small Company Stocks | $16,000 | 13% |
| Foreign Stocks | $8,000 | 6% |
| S&P 500 Index Fund | $59,000 | 46% |
| Bond Fund | $34,000 | 26% |
| Stable Value Fund | $11,000 | 9% |
| | $128,000 | 100% |

Addie's stock allocation is now 65% of her portfolio even though her deposits went in at 60%. Good for her! She has been rewarded for her allocation to stocks. But she truly likes that 60/40 mix as part of her long-term goals and volatility management, so she rebalances the portfolio to look like this:

| | | |
|---|---|---|
| Small Company Stocks | $12,800 | 10% |
| Foreign Stocks | $6,400 | 5% |
| S&P 500 Index Fund | $57,600 | 45% |
| Bond Fund | $38,400 | 30% |
| Stable Value Fund | $12,800 | 10% |
| | $128,000 | 100% |

She has been disciplined at rebalancing, and transferred 5% of her money out of stocks and into bonds or fixed income investments, bringing her balance to the target 60/40 mix (as well as to her specific desired allocations within all stock and fixed income asset classes). Now, if the stock market or a specific portion of it drops, she has already captured some gains by transferring money out of stocks to bonds when stock values were higher.

Likewise, after the stock market has a bad year, she will rebalance bond money over to the stock side of her portfolio at the time that stocks are "cheap." Then when stocks recover, she will have more invested in stocks at the beginning of the rally.

A study published in *Forbes* in 2011 examined two hypothetical investors who each put $10,000 into a 60/40 mix of stocks and bonds in 1985. One never rebalanced the portfolio, the other rebalanced annually. For the entire 25-year period from 1985 to 2010, the portfolio of the guy who rebalanced grew to $97,000, beating the other investor at $89,000. Of course, there were times when the rebalancing didn't work, such as a prolonged bull market in stocks. But the theory and the practice over the decades supported the concept of rebalancing a portfolio.

There are "balanced" fund and retirement date funds in your City of Chicago 457 plan that automatically rebalance to their targets. And you can also enroll in "Asset Rebalancing" as a feature in your plan. Or you can keep your eyes on your account and rebalance on a set schedule or just make a judgment call when you get a little or a lot off target.

## ASSET ALLOCATION AND REBALANCING MADE EASY

A generation ago an investment adviser could conduct a two-day seminar on the why's and how's of proper asset allocation, diversification, and rebalancing. Then the major mutual fund companies and plan administrators came along with new products that execute these strategies automatically—the "balanced fund" or the "retirement date" fund or something similar. Balanced funds invest in a blend of assets that is routinely rebalanced. In a target or "retirement date" fund, the investor picks an approximate date for retirement, say 2050, then invests in a fund with that 2050 retirement goal in mind. That investment fund in 2025 is fairly aggressive in terms of its allocation to equities (stocks), including higher risk small companies and foreign stocks. But as 2050 approaches, the manager switches gradually to a more conservative portfolio. And, along the way, the account is regularly rebalanced. The City of Chicago deferred compensation plan offers these balanced and retirement date funds.

## A WORD ABOUT PASSIVE INVESTING

If you don't choose a target date fund but prefer to select your own investments, a well-regarded piece of advice is to invest some or a good portion of your savings in an index fund. Let's examine the idea of an "index" and then explore the concept and advantages of an index fund. Note that the City of Chicago deferred compensation plan offers four stock index funds as investment options.

An index is a hypothetical portfolio of investments that a knowledgeable group of people believe properly reflects the performance of an entire asset class. We hear about indexes all the time. When the TV news reports that the stock market went up 40 points, what does that mean? It means that a stock index, usually 30 companies monitored by the Dow Jones Company, went up 40 points. A broader index from Standard & Poors tracks 500 large-company stocks; it is called the S&P 500 Index. When the stock market is measured over the years and decades, most observers are talking about the S&P 500. And there is an index for almost every asset class.

In 1976, the first "stock index fund" was launched, in which investor money was simply placed in each of the 500 S&P stocks. The fund did not have stock analysts researching whether any one stock, say Mobil Oil, was good deal. Mobil Oil (now Exxon) was in the index, so it was in the investment fund. Continuing, the index fund manager didn't consult economists to predict the ups and downs of the energy crisis. If 17% of the S&P 500 index companies were energy-related, then 17% of the index fund was in energy.

This is sometimes called passive investing. That phrase is used to differentiate the investment approach from an "active" manager who studies interest rates, company credit ratings, economic growth, and a zillion other factors before making an investment. The "passive" manager just sits back passively and selects securities that are in the underlying index.

This started in 1976. Today, there are trillions of dollars in index funds of all types: S&P 500, Wilshire 3000 small company index, Barclay's aggregate bond index, and many others.

Why invest in index funds? For two reasons: First, it's cheap. The fees charged against your investment balance in an index fund are the lowest available (your returns in public employee deferred compensation are always "net" of the fees paid to the investment manager). Since the index manager doesn't have to hire analysts and economists for the fund, those savings are passed on to the investor. Secondly, stock index funds, over time, produce returns comparable to or exceeding the more expensive "active" management approach.

But you may do better using active managers. Just keep the index concept in mind and do your own research into index or passive investing if the matter interests you.

## HOW SAFE IS SECTION 457 INVESTING?

Risk of loss of principle is always present unless you are directly buying US government bonds or making FDIC insured bank deposits. Everything else includes some risk, such as a company going out of business or a foreign government defaulting on its debt. Only you can do both the research and the self-analysis to decide how much risk you are willing to take. The good news is that the various types of investment risk—credit, market, interest rates, foreign currency, whatever—are unchanged inside the Section 457 umbrella. Investing in the Vanguard Life Strategy Growth Fund directly or through your 457 plan is no different, risk or otherwise.

How about out-and-out theft? Remember Bernie Madoff? He took investors' money, did *not* buy the securities or options that he promised, and then created phony statements to indicate that he had made proper investments. Meanwhile he was living the good life on his investors' cash. Could that happen in a major 457 administrator's operation or in the underlying mutual funds or accounts? Never say never, but it's just highly unlikely. All these operations have the proper trust account and custodian players in place (a custodian is a bank that holds the investments—the investment manager does not have access to the actual securities). If you have any doubts, talk to your plan representative.

We have a lot of confidence that the assets are safe. We know of no money that has been lost in modern day 457 savings other than from routine and expected investment volatility. The two principal authors of this book used the City of Chicago plan and a suburban government plan to build on their personal retirement security.

## CLOSING THOUGHTS ON INVESTING

Deferred compensation plans give a public employee the opportunity to build a diversified portfolio with an amazingly small starting investment. For example, a new participant in deferred compensation might have his or her first $20 deposit put one-fourth each into an S&P 500 index fund, a small company stock fund, an international stock fund, and a government bond fund. Is this really possible with just $20?—a $5 investment into foreign stocks and the rest into a diversified stock and bond portfolio? Yes, it is possible—in employer-sponsored deferred compensation.

Allocation of retirement investment among asset classes is your most important decision after the decision to save, and before the decision of which specific mutual funds to pick. If you are unsure of how to invest your money, do some research or seek investment advice from a professional. Investing in a 457 plan is very similar to investing in a 401(k) plan, so investment advisers, good ones, should be able to help you.

A recommendation is either of two excellent books by William Bernstein: *The Intelligent Asset Allocator* and *The Four Pillars of Investing: Lessons for Building a Winning Portfolio*. Dr. Bernstein is a neurologist who at some point began to fancy himself to be an investment expert. Turned out he was right. You can use the excellent information in either of these books to assist you in your deferred compensation investment plan.

One way that a 401(k) plan and a 457 plan are dissimilar is that the 401(k) private sector employee may receive an employer match. The trade-off usually is that the private sector worker probably does not have a defined benefit pension like you do at CPD or CFD. But since you do have a DB plan, here's something to remember: your fixed pension acts in many ways like a bond investment. If you consider that when you decide on an asset allocation in deferred compensation, you'll put considerably more in the domestic and foreign stock markets. The fact that your defined benefit pension plan pays out a guaranteed fixed amount each month allows you to be more aggressive in the stock market with personal savings.

Timing the market doesn't work. If you think you can *consistently* move out of stocks at the top and go back in at the bottom of the market, get out of public safety and make yourself a billionaire.

# TURNING 457 MONEY INTO RETIREMENT INCOME

Section 457 money is deferred for retirement purposes. You do not have access to the funds until you either separate from employment (quit or retire) or have an unforeseeable financial emergency. The rules regarding withdrawal for an unforeseeable emergency are very strict. The emergency must be something for which a reasonable person would not budget and cannot be dealt with using savings outside of the Section 457 plan. Imminent foreclosure, eviction, uninsured medical or funeral expenses or an uninsured casualty loss are examples of unforeseeable emergencies. *This is a high barrier to access.* Don't plan on being able to get the money until you leave the job or reach retirement age. Deferred compensation is a supplemental retirement plan; consider it as such. Note that the City of Chicago Deferred Compensation Plan has a loan provision for pre-tax dollars only.

## BEFORE YOU NEED THE MONEY, SHOULD YOU STAY WHERE YOU ARE OR USE THE IRA ROLLOVER OPTION?

At the time you retire, you may not need any of the proceeds of your Section 457 account. If you leave the money in place, your balance continues to grow on a tax-deferred basis. If you don't want to begin drawing the money at retirement, the only decision to be made is whether or not you want to leave your balance with your employer's deferred compensation plan or roll it over into an existing or new Individual Retirement Account (IRA).

> **There is a good case for leaving the money where it is** if you are satisfied with the Chicago 457 plan: the investment options that are offered, the fees, the customer service provided by the administrator, the continued oversight by your employer and union, and the opportunity to discuss the plan with your active and retired coworkers. If you are happy with the plan that helped you build a pretty good nest egg, why change?

**There is a case for rolling the money into an IRA** if you are not totally satisfied with your employer's plan, you'd like to consolidate your investments with another company or advisor, or you want to make some distributions to charities though an IRA permitted "Qualified Charitable Distribution (QCD)."

A word of caution is in order regarding the 10% penalty that is paid when money is withdrawn from an IRA before age 59-1/2. Your municipal 457 plan does not have a 10% penalty for withdrawal before age 59-1/2. **Whenever you take out Section 457 money you pay only the tax.** But IRAs and a new employer's 401(k) plan *do* have such a penalty. If you roll Section 457 money into a plan that has such a rule, your 457 money will be subject to a 10% penalty if withdrawn before age 59-1/2. For this reason, it might be better to leave your balance with the deferred compensation plan administrator at least until you are ready to begin distributions or at least until after age 59-1/2.

There is a lot of good information available from general sources to help you make the rollover/don't-rollover decision.

Rolling your money over into an IRA and then converting the IRA to a Roth IRA is a related strategy, again beyond the scope of this book. But there is considerable information and advice available on this subject.

## WHEN YOU NEED THE MONEY

Prior to age 73, you have considerable flexibility on withdrawal of the funds. As retirement approaches, you should be in contact with your plan administrator to go over your options. Taking all your money out at once is certainly allowed. This is the so-called "lump sum option," but you'll possibly skyrocket into a high tax bracket if you do this. Not a good idea.

You may want to choose a series of systematic withdrawals paid on a set schedule (month, quarter, year). While the money is being paid out, your balance stays invested as you have directed.

Or you may choose some other schedule. When that time comes, check out your options. Again, your balance always stays invested as you directed while you are drawing out the money.

There is a lot written about how much a retiree can safely draw out of a defined contribution retirement plan and not run out of money during his or her life. Since public employee deferred compensation plans are supplemental to a pension (in the case of Illinois, a modified-inflation-adjusted pension), the rate of withdrawal is not critical as it is for a person in a 401(k)-only retirement environment. Again, there is a lot written on this subject and it is easily available.

## REQUIRED MINIMUM DISTRIBUTIONS

However, beginning at age 73, if you are no longer working for the City of Chicago, you must begin withdrawals that meet or exceed so-called Required Minimum Distributions (RMD). Essentially the RMD is an annual amount calculated with the intent that most of the account balance will be withdrawn during the remaining life of the participant. The plan administrator can advise you of how the RMD schedule will work and may have an on-line RMD Calculator to assist you in your planning. You can also look directly at the approved IRS schedule at irs.gov or simply Google "RMD table."

Here is a quick example. At the date of publication of this book, an age 73 retiree with a $200,000 account balance must withdraw at least $7,550 that year. At age 81, an account balance of $200,000 would trigger a minimum withdrawal of $10,300. These numbers will vary in the future.

If you do not live long enough to draw out a large part of your balance, there is no penalty associated with this. Any balance left when you die passes to your heirs and the tax liability is transferred to the next owner (possibly with different withdrawal rules). Your beneficiary pays the tax when the money is withdrawn.

Work closely with your IRA custodian or 457 plan administrator to ensure you are following RMD rules.

## THE ANNUITY OPTION

Before or after age 73, there is the opportunity to purchase an **annuity** to pay you (or you and your spouse) a monthly amount for life. Under this option, your balance does *not* stay invested as you direct. The annuity company takes all the money in exchange for the promise to pay the annuity each month as long as you live. If you live a short time, they win. If you live until 102, *you* win. There are also some variations where you can guarantee that a minimum number of payments will be made to your survivors even if you don't live a long time. Examples of specific types of payments follow later.

When you buy an annuity, you are really transferring investment risk and mortality risk (*i.e.*, how long you are going to live) to an insurance company. Some private sector retirees may want to do this. If a person was self-employed and sold a business in retirement for $3 million, he or she might reasonably consider using some of that money to buy an annuity. Since that retiree does not have a pension, the annuity that is purchased acts in many ways just like a pension.

**But not many public safety retirees choose annuities to withdraw money from their deferred compensation plan.** You already have a guaranteed income for life (the fire or police pension) with some level of inflation protection. You likely also have a small Social Security benefit coming. So, it's reasonably safe for a police or fire pensioner to accept the investment and mortality risk of their deferred compensation account as opposed to transferring that risk to an insurance company (and incurring the insurance contract's attendant fees and profits).

But if you want to check out an annuity option, check it out!

## DEFERRED COMPENSATION SUMMARY

A public employee can place a considerable amount of personal savings into a deferred compensation account. This approach will beat savings outside the account in the long term. There are a broad range of diversified asset classes that can be chosen and mixed to create excellent long-term gains. Participants should understand these investments well enough to make appropriate allocation decisions. If you are not in that position, you can improve your own knowledge and/or work with the deferred compensation company or a personal advisor to assist you. Rebalancing your account regularly or even from time to time adds value. Deferred compensation accounts can also be put on a sort of "automatic pilot" as there are opportunities for preset, age-appropriate investing and rebalancing. There is a lot of flexibility in withdrawing the money, but moderately sized withdrawals must occur at age 73.

## THOUGHTS THAT DIDN'T FIT ANYWHERE ELSE

Section 457 plans are very popular where they have been introduced. And, these plans were popular under the *old* rules, which restricted withdrawal options and treated account balances as the property of an employer. With the 1996 and 2000 reforms, interest in 457 plan participation grew. The tax break on contributions, access to the broad investment markets for a small deposit and the convenience of payroll deduction make these plans an excellent "third leg" of the retirement stool.

Police and fire personnel should take pride in the fact that they and their co-workers are the largest savers among public employees. This is most likely due to a tradition of taking care of each other. You depend on your coworkers at a working fire or a crime-in-progress. You look out for each other then and you look out for the young officers and firefighters by encouraging them to participate in deferred compensation. Keep up the good work.

The dollars that go into deferred compensation will end up in competition with other expense and savings needs: buying a house, saving for kids' college, and other requirements of life. It's hard to max out every year and still feed your family. So don't worry when your first child is born and your spouse cuts back at work. You will probably need to drop your contribution to deferred compensation. Keep everything in balance. But remember that magical time value of compounded earnings. Don't let deferred compensation sit too long on a back burner. The best approach: start deferring as soon as you are eligible.

## WHAT ELSE CAN YOU DO TO IMPROVE YOUR DEFERRED SAVINGS?

There are a range of further actions you can consider. Or not. Many of the readers already have a good grasp of their deferred compensation personal savings plan.

Of course, if you are not saving in deferred compensation, strongly consider joining the plan.

If you are enrolled in deferred compensation and would like to improve this leg of your retirement income, you can do a little or a lot. Reread this chapter. Visit your plan administrator's website (chicagodeferredcomp.com) or review the written plan material. Consider the two recommended books by Dr. Bernstein or find something similar. Maybe a relative or a friend has a decent financial planning or retirement book.

The City of Chicago HR Department offers a series of videos to assist employees in preparing for retirement. One of the videos is an excellent presentation from Nationwide on "Approaching Retirement—Deferred Compensation." Go to the HR department website under Chicago.gov, click on Government then click on Human Resources. At their home page, under Related Links, click on "Retirement Information for City Employees."

Rebalance your account if it hasn't been done since the 1990s. Be sure you understand your investments and statements. If you don't understand them, plan a meeting with the deferred compensation representative. Take ownership.

## SECTION ENDNOTES

To arrive at the 23.1% tax rate imputed for "Tim's" savings outside of deferred compensation, the following was used: a blended the capital gains/dividend rate for three-quarters of his investment earnings with a typical top rate of 28%, then added 4.95 percentage points for Illinois tax.

# APPENDIX

# A

# CONTRIBUTORS

**Michael K. Lappe, *IPPFA and Retired Chicago Police***
Mike is a former Chicago Police officer who retired from CPD after more than 38 years of experience. Critically injured in a shooting incident, Mike rehabbed himself and returned to limited duty. He currently serves as an elected retirement board trustee for the Chicago police pension fund and is a past adjunct professor in criminal justice. He has a master's degree in public safety administration and is considered an expert in disability pensions for police officers. Mike is a part-time staff associate for the Illinois Public Pension Fund Association (IPPFA).

**Daniel W. Ryan, *IPPFA and Retired***
Dan is retired from careers as a municipal finance director and union benefit administrator and is a longtime trustee of the Skokie police pension fund. His research and writings on Social Security and public pensions have been referenced in pension fund newsletters and newspapers nationwide, including the *Wall Street Journal*. He is a part-time project coordinator for IPPFA.

**Anthony Martin, *Chicago Fire Department***
Tony is an active-duty Battalion Chief and CFD and is a long-term trustee of the Chicago Fire and Annuity Benefit Fund. He is a licensed attorney and the author of the fire pension fund's "Summary of Benefits" on which the CFD pension material in this book is based.

**James McNamee, *IPPFA***
Born in Chicago, Jim McNamee began his career in law enforcement in 1979 as a police officer for the Village of Barrington. In 1983, Mr. McNamee was elected to the Barrington Police Pension Board as a trustee. During his term as trustee, he quickly saw the need for training and education for all trustees of pension boards. Taking action, Mr. McNamee went to work to form the Illinois Police Pension Fund Association now known as the Illinois Public Pension Fund Association.

***IPPFA Association Office***
Administrative assistance was provided by IPPFA office staff Julie Guy, Mandy Paciorkowski, and Madeline Lusted.

***Additional Acknowledgments***
The Trustees and professional staff of the Chicago fire and police pension funds provided valuable information for this book and their help is greatly appreciated. The cover photo was provided by Frank Alatorre, CPD.

# APPENDIX

# B

# "DON'T LET EVIL WIN"

MY PARTNER ON THIS BOOK PROJECT, Mike Lappe, is a now retired, decorated Chicago police officer.

Several years ago he shared his story of injury and recovery with the IPPFA membership. His essay, "Don't Let EVIL Win," is reprinted here.

~Dan Ryan
Project Coordinator, IPPFA
Trustee, Skokie Police Pension Fund

# DON'T LET EVIL WIN

## TURN TRAGEDY INTO VICTORY

By Michael Lappe, CPD (retired)

LET ME BEGIN BY TELLING YOU that I am deeply humbled to have been asked to address this subject with you, my fellow law enforcement officers and first responders from throughout Illinois.

First, a message from Dr. Lawrence N. Blum, *Ph.D.*, an expert in law enforcement trauma issues:

> I have come to believe that if surviving officers truly want to honor those who have fallen in the line of duty, then they must learn the important lessons that come from their experiences and commit themselves to the quest for mastery in law enforcement: *turn tragedy into victory.*

So now the question is: how does an individual turn tragedy into victory while at the same time enjoying the gift and a better quality of life? After I was asked to address this topic, one day after my office closed, I stayed late when I was alone, having peace and quiet. I began to reflect on my life-changing incident. As I examined so many of the components of this complex topic, I kept asking myself: what worked, what did not, who stood beside me? Please keep this in mind that I am not here to brag or boast, but to pass along a true-life incident that happened to me, just as it could have happened to anyone of you here today. Your life could change in an instant, no matter how cautious you are, as you strive to be the best version of yourself in your personal and professional lives.

## My Incident

In 1988 with eight years of police service under my belt, I considered myself to be a seasoned officer having worked some of the meanest streets of Chicago's west side. Realizing that danger and *Evil's* ugly face was prevalent all around, I decided to request a transfer to a "slower" district which a few years later was granted. At 32 years of age and beginning to raise a family, I knew I had made the right decision.

On Sunday, April 24, 1988, my day started out doing the normal family stuff. Church, then home and a quick breakfast with the wife and kids. Our daughters Molly and Erin were 3 and 1 ½ years old. With our daughters being so young, things continually changed without notice.

At mid-afternoon I took our 3-year-old swimming at the local YMCA as our other daughter and mom took a well-deserved nap. Lots of fun diving off the board and showing-off was the rule this day. Life as we were living it was great! By late in the afternoon it was time to head home, help out with a few chores, then dress for work. I was on the 6 pm to 2 am crime-fighting tactical shift.

At 5:30 just before heading out the door, hugs and kisses were given to the wife and kids with simple words: I love you guys, be good for mommy. We love you too daddy, see you in the morning.

Roll call began at 6 pm in the 016th district tactical office. Shortly thereafter we "hit the streets." I was part of an eight-man plain clothes unit that aggressively responded to narcotic sales, in-progress felony calls or backing up a beat officer. A tactical officer's training is designed to fend off an assault and take control of any type of incident.

At 7:15 pm we responded as a back-up unit at a domestic call.

These calls are no different in a suburban or small-town setting than they are in Chicago, or to anywhere a first responder may be summoned for that matter. I'm confidant saying any officer can relate that over time these calls for service become somewhat routine.

As we arrived at the 4800 W. Ainslie call-for-service location, the dispatcher relayed information from an interview quickly completed with the 911 caller, who happened to be the victim and the 72-year-old mother of the suspect. This interview took place outside the home on the sidewalk. The victim/mother spoke broken English, which started the chain of events which caused the first responders to enter the residence not knowing what to expect. The only information from the victim was that her son was "crazy."

I entered the residence with two uniformed officers as my partner walked around to the rear of the house in the event the subject ran; we would be prepared to take him into custody. After all, I was the 8-year veteran, my partner had 15 and the two uniformed officers had 20 plus years each!

As the three of us entered the front room the subject yelled out from the rear of the home: "GET OUT OF MY HOUSE NOW."

This straightforward situation now just took a turn for the worse. The offender just declared himself an active adversarial.

Calmly, but firmly, I replied that we just wanted to speak to him to see what's been going on here with his mother. As I cautiously approached the kitchen area from a narrow hallway, my duty weapon un-holstered and firmly gripped in my hand, my experience told me to look by the kitchen table, that is where he'll be sitting. However, we all misjudged this one. In a fraction of a second the subject ambushed us as he sprang up from behind a stove. He immediately fired at me from less than four feet away, striking me in the throat. As I fell backwards on the floor in the hallway, other components of police training took over as I tried desperately to return fire from laying on the floor, but eventually my weapon fell from my hand. I was now helpless. An ensuing gun battle took place over me as I lay there having been instantly paralyzed.

There was no more police training to rely on.

*EVIL* got me.

## Still Alive, But in Trouble

I was now thinking about my wife and daughters as the air in my body was escaping out of my windpipe. Responding units secured the interior and began to remove me. I told my teammates to take me outside to die, don't keep me in here. My last message before I lapsed into unconsciousness was for them to tell Mary and my girls that I love them. I knew this wasn't good. I knew I only had a moment left before I would be gone.

Days later I awoke in the intensive care unit at Lutheran General Hospital. I knew right away that it was serious. I looked at my hands and arms which could move, but not my legs from the waist down. I could not speak. I had tubes inserted in every hole God gave me (plus a few more to boot!). My wife was at my side along with a friend and I signaled for a pen and paper.

I wrote only two words with a question mark. "Bad guy?" After being told that *EVIL* had killed himself in a standoff with police, I believe my healing process began right then and there.

During the next 4½ months of hospital confinement, I experienced a few life-threatening setbacks. From blood filling my lungs after the throat wound internally opened, to the pulmonary embolism for which another "code blue" was called.

Almost five months is a long time to think about what had happened. How am I going to survive this ordeal? I kept telling myself as I do to this very day, I'm not going to let *EVIL win*. If I had left a profession that I love so much and ended up as an unproductive person at the age of 33, who knows what my and my family's future would have held. I maintained all my upper body strength as I was told early on that the probability of me ever walking again was very marginal.

The last thing that a "copper" anywhere wants to hear is: NO, you can't do this or NO you can't do that.

With the grace of God, extensive physical therapy from dedicated medical personnel and my family coaching me, I am here today, alive and walking (sort of!). My wife Mary has been my loudest cheerleader despite my own faults and stubbornness. I was always too proud to say "thank you" for all she did and sacrificed for me and the kids as we went through those horrific times. A few years later she encouraged me to enroll in night school while she continued to raise the kids and worked full time in her nursing profession. I cannot thank her or our children enough.

## But More Trouble Was Coming

During my extended time period of home recuperation, I struggled to challenge myself mentally and physically. These endless days gave me the opportunity to eventually re-start doing light home chores. Cutting the lawn again and its fresh smell were awesome. I managed this task by taking small steps, using a quad cane for balance, and telling myself I could do it, don't be a wimp!

On a lighter note: one thing I was not prepared for was having my toddler daughters insisting we play dolls and dress up while they put curlers in my hair! All this dad could do was smile at them, at the same time thinking, I've got to get back to work: FAST!

But this fun hid a problem. Let me be brutally honest here.

Something else happened to me that at the time to which I was totally oblivious. I began to treat my wife almost as if she was the one who shot me. I became very short tempered and started to be ticked off at the world. The weeks and months became harder and harder for me as I was now having the "dream" reliving the entire event of me being shot and how I wish I were the one who shot first.

But what really became scary was when my wife and I needed to go out in the car, I sat in the passenger seat wearing two AFO leg braces, special shoes, using two quad canes and having a loaded .45 caliber handgun situated between my upper legs. I had become paranoid that someone would walk up to the car and begin shooting at me. Believe me, I was ready to begin shooting if someone had walked up to the passenger side window. My wife was constantly crying her eyes out begging me to seek help. Unbeknown to me, I look back and now realize that this was PTSD that had snuck into my body.

It was a few days later that I started to ask myself just what the hell are you doing with a loaded pistol at the ready? That's when I realized that yes, I do need to seek some professional help. I had to do what was right for Mary and the kids. I could not risk ever losing them. Losing them to me meant that if I ended up in a tavern feeling sorry for myself, and Mary taking the kids away from me, that the guy who shot me would have won (even though he went to the morgue the night of the shooting). He would have taken the life of a police officer just as he intended to do, only in another way.

## Changing Attitudes

During the mid-1980s, there was a dramatic change in policing throughout the country. It used to be that when an officer involved shooting occurred the profession's response was "let's stop after work for a few cold ones," or "suck it up kid, just part of the job." I don't have any statistics to share with you, but history suggests that some officers found the end of their life at the end of a gun barrel that could be directly related to a traumatic work-related event.

Since then and fast-forward to today's modern policing: more and more agencies are beginning to recognize PTSD and it's no more "have a couple of drinks, you'll be fine." Professional help has become the norm.

Life can be so unfair, unpredictable, emotional, and by all accounts taken away in a flash. When a first responder suffers the misfortune or aftermath of a tragic event, he or she always asks the question to themselves, why did this happen to me? I'm a good person. I should be at work or with my loved ones, helping the kids with their homework, being a husband, a wife, a daughter, a son: *EVIL* should be in this hospital, *NOT ME!*

The reality is, as good, honest, heroic, and righteous as we may try to be, if you were to experience an incident compounded with an extended stay in either a hospital or a care giving facility, friends and family become less and less visible for visits as time marches on.

The fact is human nature tells us that your network of friends and family are starting to move along in their lives while yours is on hold. This is where a first responder's courage and warrior instincts need to kick in.

Again, I don't need to remind you that *EVIL* should not and cannot prevail. Physically, you may survive, but mentally, emotionally you now realize just how close you may have come to dying as the full scope of your event hits home. This may take a toll on you with flashbacks for the short-term period or the rest of your life. When I look back, I can picture myself with tears rolling down my face asking how am I going to provide for my wife and daughters with a life confined to a wheelchair? In my situation, I recovered enough to ambulate and regain a quality of life that may not be perfect physically, but knowing the guy that shot me will never win to split my family apart.

## A Few Last Points

Lastly, on one's road to recovery, don't fall victim to:

- Substance abuse
- Excessive alcohol consumption
- Gambling addiction
- Domestic violence
- Emotional distress
- Or perhaps other critical situation(s)

Don't fall prey to these demons.

Celebrate the good things in life.
Take nothing for granted.
That's the rule!

MICHAEL LAPPE is a retired Chicago Police officer who retired from CPD on a service pension after more than 36 years of experience. Critically injured in a shooting incident, Mike rehabbed himself and returned to full duty. He has served as an elected retirement board trustee and as an adjunct professor in criminal justice. He has a master's degree in Public Safety Administration and is considered an expert in disability pensions for police officers. Mike now services as a part-time staff member at the Illinois Public Pension Fund Association and as an instructor in the IPPFA's *Saving Blue Lives* program.

# APPENDIX

# C

# "HELPS" TAX BREAK RETIREE MEDICAL INSURANCE PAYMENTS

RETIRED POLICE AND FIREFIGHTERS/EMTs may be able to reduce their taxable earnings by up to $3,000 for medical insurance premiums paid during a calendar year. This is allowable under the Healthcare Enhancement for Local Public Safety Retirees Act, or the "HELPS" Retiree Act.

When initially passed, there was a requirement that the premium be deducted from the retiree's pension check in order to qualify for HELPS tax break. That is no longer the case following the adoption of the federal Secure 2.0 retirement law. Premiums paid directly to the insurer for health, accident, or long-term care insurance qualify for the credit. Note that the tax break is not available to surviving spouses.

The $3,000 reduction does not appear on the 1099R form from the pension fund. The retiree must claim the reduction on his or her personal 1040 tax form on Line 5B or similar adjustment. Instructions on claiming the reduction are included in IRS Publication 575, page 7 with update on page 2. As this is not a simple matter, you may want to consult with a tax preparer to properly claim the reduction.

Note that married couples where both the parties are retired police/fire/ EMS may take a reduction in income of up to $6,000.

More information on this subject is available at IPPFA.org.
Click on Bulletins, then select the HELPS Retiree Insurance Bulletin.

Made in the USA
Monee, IL
04 November 2026

67380145R00066